MODERN
MILITARY
HELICOPTERS

PAUL BEAVER

MODERN
MILITARY
HELICOPTERS

PAUL BEAVER

Patrick Stephens
Wellingborough, Northamptonshire

First published in 1987

British Library Cataloguing in Publication Data

Beaver, Paul
Military helicopters.
1. Military helicopters — Handbooks,
manuals, etc.
I. Title
623.74'6047   UG1230
ISBN 0-85059-893-1

Cover illustrations
Front *The AH-64A Apache is the world's first advanced
attack helicopter and entered service in April 1986*
(McDonnell Douglas Helicopters).

Back *MBB's BO 105P is the Federal German Army's
front line defence against invasion from the East* (MBB).

*Patrick Stephens Limited is part of the
Thorsons Publishing Group,
Wellingborough, Northamptonshire, NN8 2RQ, England*

Printed in Great Britain by R. J. Acford, Chichester, Sussex

3   5   7   9   10   8   6   4   2

CONTENTS

INTRODUCTION AND ACKNOWLEDGEMENTS

'Helicopters are my top priority and it is inconceivable to imagine a military operation without them, especially for command and control, control of aircraft and logistical support — but more than ever they have become a fighting arm in their own right with an incredible capability of destroying thirty main battle tanks (a Warsaw Pact battalion) in less than two minutes. With its flexibility and element of surprise, the helicopter is vital and many other things will go to the wall before helicopters.'

General Sir Martin Farndale
Commander Northern Army Group (NATO) and Commander-in-Chief, British Army of the Rhine, Winchester, England, July 1986

Over the last few years, there has been an increasingly visible and important use of military helicopters on the battlefields and high seas of the world. There is no little doubt that the vehicle is a vital element not only of the land battle as seen by General Farndale but also at sea.

Recent events such as the Falklands conflict with those dramatic rescues from *Sir Galahad* and *Sir Tristram*, the Grenada invasion by the United States, battles in the Iraq-Iran war and the highly publicized Westland Helicopters affair have all contributed to the increased awareness of the tactical value of the helicopter in war and as a viable part of a deterrent force. Today there are some 28,000 military and para-military helicopters in the world — nearly half of them in the United States forces — and they can no longer be considered as just a workhorse, they are a direct fire weapon, night or day, on land or at sea.

I am grateful to the following people for their kind assistance in telling a little more of the helicopter's story: Jean-Louis Espes (Aerospatiale), Bianca Corbella (Agusta), Carl Harris, Dick Tipton and Marty Reisch (Bell), Bob Torgerson (Boeing), Bruce Goulding (Kaman), Rob Mack and Hal Klopper (McDonnell Douglas), Christina Gotzhein (MBB), Jim Bowman and Jim Ventrilio (Sikorsky) and Ian Woodward (Westland) from the manufacturers, and also Major General David Goodman, Brigadier David Canterbury and Colonel Keith Robson (British Army Air Corps), Hauptmann Wolfgang Prskawetz (Federal German Army) and Lieutenant Commander Cy Beattie (Royal Navy Fleet Air Arm). In addition, I must thank Alexander Shephard, publisher, and the staff of *Defence Helicopter World* for kind permission to use some of the line drawing illustrations from the magazine and to Ian Commin for preparing the remaining drawings.

Paul Beaver
Old Basing, Hampshire, December 1986

TODAY'S MILITARY HELICOPTERS

The following 56 major types of helicopter are in service around the world in every role in which this air vehicle can perform. The eight major western world manufacturers are all well represented as well as the two Soviet design bureaux and several specialist manufacturers in the United States. To understand the data as presented the following notes will be of use:

Max cont power This indicates the power required of the engine(s) for normal service flying which may be lower than the initial take-off power, especially at the maximum take-off weight.
Length The length quoted is the fuselage only.
Width This is the widest track of the helicopter's fuselage/ undercarriage.
HIGE Hover in Ground Effect is the use of the ground to provide extra lift in a cushion of air.
HOGE Hover Out of Ground Effect is the action of operating the helicopter away from any possible extra lift from the ground.
Range This figure equates to standard day conditions, for sea level flight of clean helicopter.
NA This indicates that the relevant information is not available.

AEROSPATIALE

AEROSPATIALE ALOUETTE II SERIES

First flight March 12 1955; **Operational** 1957

SE 3130 Alouette II

Engine 1 × Turbomeca Artouste II C6 360 shp (derated from 530 shp); **Crew** 1 pilot; **Passengers** 4; **Max take-off weight** 1,600 kg (3,527 lb); **Payload** 705 kg (1,554 lb); **Empty weight** 895 kg (1,973 lb); **External load** 500 kg (1,102 lb); **Length** 9.7 m (31.82 ft); **Width** 2.4 m (7.8 ft); **Rotor diameter** 10.2 m (33.46 ft); **Height** 2.75 m (9.84 ft); **Max speed** 100 kt (185 km/h); **Max cruise speed** 90 kt (165 km/h); **Service ceiling** 2,250 m (7,382 ft); **Rate of climb** 4.7 m/sec (925 ft/min); **HIGE** 1,650 m (5,400 ft); **HOGE** 920 m (3,018 ft); **Range** 600 km (324 nm); **Weapons** 2 × ASW torpedoes or 4 × AS 11 missiles or 7.62 mm GPMG.

SA 313B Alouette II

Post-1957 designation for Alouette II

Practising for the World Helicopter Championships, a Federal German Heeresflieger Alouette II helicopter (Heeresflieger).

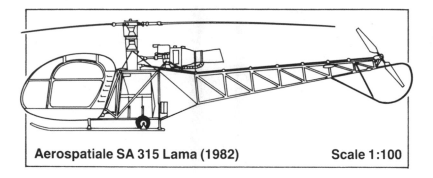

Aerospatiale SA 315 Lama (1982)   **Scale 1:100**

SA 315B Lama

Details as for SE 3130 except: **Engine** Turbomeca Artouste IIIB 562 shp (derived from 870 shp); **Max take-off weight** 1,951 kg (4,300 lb); **Payload** 923 kg (2,034 lb); **Empty weight** 1,028 kg (2,266 lb); **External load** 1,134 kg (2,500 lb); **Length** 10.2 m (33.6 ft); **Rotor diameter** 11.0 m (36.2 ft); **Height** 3.1 m (10.17 ft); **Max speed** 113 kt (209 km/h); **Cruise speed** 103 kt (191 km/h); **Service ceiling** 5,401 m (17,720 ft); **Rate of climb** 5.5 m/sec (1,082 ft/min); **HIGE** 5,049 m (16,565 ft); **HOGE** 4,602 m (15,100 ft); **Range** 515 km (278 nm); **Weapons** usually unarmed

HAL Cheetah

Licence-built in India (see SA 315B details)

Helibras HB 315B Gaviao

Licence-built in Brazil (see SA 315B details)

SA 318C Alouette II

Details as for SE 3130 except: **Engine** Turbomeca Astazou IIA 360 shp (derived from 530 shp); **Max speed** 111 kt (205 km/h); **Cruise speed** 92 kt (170 km/h); **Service ceiling** 3,300 m (10,827 ft); **Rate of climb** 6.6 m/sec (1,300 ft/min); **HIGE** 1,520 m (4,987 ft); **HOGE** 950 m (3,117 ft); **Range** 350 km (189 nm)

Originally designed for agricultural operations, the Alouette II series was produced from 1957 until 1975; during that time it was supplied by Sud-Est (later Aerospatiale) to 46 nations for battlefield, naval and training roles. It has been operational in the Algerian, Biafran and Lebanese conflicts, mainly for liaison and communication tasks.

It is constructed of a light metal frame, with a large plexiglass

SA 316B Alouette III helicopter carrying out a training flight from Toulon, southern France. Note the flotation bags (Aerospatiale).

cockpit and the main rotor has three metal blades. The helicopter can be mounted on traditional lightweight skids or floats, depending upon the operation to be carried out.

The Lama/Cheetah/Gaviao series was designed to give greater power for hot/high operations and the helicopter is a hybrid between the Alouette II and III. The Indian Air Force requirement for a helicopter to operate in the Himalayan mountains during the Indo-Sino War led to the Lama, which was built under licence by HAL in Bangalore as the Cheetah; this helicopter was one of the first to transfer to the Indian Army Air Corps in 1986. In South America, the Gaviao has been built for the Brazilian, Bolivian and Chilean armed forces.

AEROSPATIALE ALOUETTE III SERIES

First flight February 28 1959; **Operational** 1960

SE 3160 Alouette III

Engine 1 × Turbomeca Artouste IIIB 570 shp (derated from 870 shp); **Crew** 1 pilot/1 crewman; **Passengers** 5-6; **Max take-off weight** 2,200 kg (4,850 lb); **Payload** 1,095 kg (2,413 lb); **Empty weight** 1,122 kg (2,474 lb); **External load** 750 kg (1,650 lb); **Length** 10.2 m (33.38 ft); **Width** 2.6 m (8.53 ft); **Rotor diameter** 11.02 m (36.15 ft); **Height** 3.0 m (9.84 ft); **Max speed** 113 kt (210 km/h); **Cruise speed** 106 kt (197 km/h); **Service ceiling** 4,250 m (13,943 ft); **Rate of climb** 4 m/sec (800 ft/min); **HIGE** 2,880 m (9,449 ft); **HOGE** 1,520 m (4,987 ft); **Range** 480 km (259

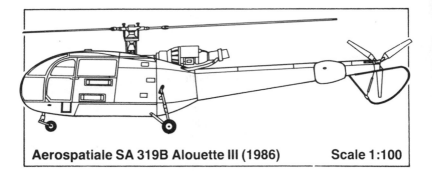

Aerospatiale SA 319B Alouette III (1986) | **Scale 1:100**

nm); **Weapons** 4 × AS 11 or 2 × AS 12; 2 × 7.62 mm; 1 × Browning 20 mm; 2 × 68 mm rocket pods.

SA 316B Alouette III
Post-1970 name for Alouette III with Artouste

SA 319B Alouette III
Details as for SE 3160 except: **Engine** 1 × Turbomeca Astazou XIVB 592 shp (derated from 870 shp); **Max take-off weight** 2,250 kg (4,960 lb); **Empty weight** 1,146 kg (2,527 lb); **Max speed** 118 kt (220 km/h); **Cruise speed** 105 kt (195 km/h); **Service ceiling** 4,100 m (13,450 ft); **Rate of climb** 4.5 m/sec (886 ft/min); **HIGE** 3,100 m (10,170 ft); **HOGE** 1,700 m (5,575 ft); **Range** 630 km (340 nm); **Weapons** as above plus 2 × Mk46 ASW torpedoes or 1 × Mk46 + MAD.

IAR 316B
Roumanian-built version, still in production

HAL Chetak
Indian-built version of SA 319B, still in production

The Alouette III was developed from the Alouette II by Sud-Est, which merged with other French aerospace companies to become Aerospatiale in 1970. The helicopter's fuselage is constructed of lightweight steel framing, clad with sheet metal with a semi-monocoque tail boom; the three main rotor blades are metal.

The naval version can mount a weather radar in the nose and carry a rescue winch for SAR missions. It is embarked in Chilean and Indian naval vessels, the latter have reported fitted MAD (Magnetic Anomoly Detector) gear, which can be carried by those helicopters of the type still operational with the French Aeronavale. Emergency floats can also be fitted.

Active in several conflicts, including the bush wars of Southern Africa (Rhodesia, Angola, Mozambique and South-West Africa Namibia), the helicopter has acquitted itself well, especially in terms of its operational reliability. Local modifications have included 'elephant ears'—sand filters for the engines—and the fitting of a variety of weapons, including rocket launchers, machine guns and cannon. The Rhodesians and South Africans have successfully used the helicopters in search and destroy missions, whilst an Argentine Alouette III was active in the invasion of South Georgia in 1982, being damaged by the Royal Marines. Nearly fifty armed forces operate the helicopter and it has been assembled under licence in Switzerland and India, being built under licence in India and Roumania. Production in France ceased in 1983 after over 1,400 had been built.

The French ALAT's battlefield version is being withdrawn from service and replaced by the SA 341/342 Gazelle, but other services will continue to use the helicopter until at least 2000.

ALOUETTE III DERIVATIVES

Armscor/Atlas XH-1 Alpha

First flight 3 February 1985; **Operational** 1987/88; **Engine** 1 × gas turbine; **Crew** 1 pilot, 1 co-pilot/gunner; **Passengers** 0; **Max take-off weight** est 2,200 kg (4,850 lb); **Payload** 1,000 kg (2,205 lb); **Empty weight** 1,400 kg (3,086 lb); **External load** N A; **Length** 10.2 m (33.4 ft); **Width** 2.6 m (8.53 ft); **Rotor diameter** 11.02 m (36.15 ft); **Height** 3.5 m (11.48 ft); **Max speed** 115 kt (213 km/h); **Max cruise speed** 105 kt (194 km/h); **Service ceiling** 3,200 m (10,499 ft); **Rate of climb** 4.6 m/sec (900 ft/min); **HIGE** N A; **HOGE** N A; **Range** 400 km (216 nm); **Weapons** 1 × GAI 20 mm chin-mounted cannon.

In March 1986 when the first XH-1 Alpha was shown to the press in South Africa, it was not a truly surprising event because there had been considerable speculation about the development of an attack helicopter in the Republic. Although obviously based on the Alouette III helicopter, the South African Air Force maintains that the Alpha is a completely developed airframe and systems fit, including the 20 mm cannon with its integrated helmet-mounted sight. Although the engine and transmission are not locally developed they contain many locally manufactured components.

Left *The first helicopter designed and developed in South Africa is the Armscor/Atlas XH-1 Alpha, based on the Alouette III* (SAAF).

Right *Another Alouette III derivative, the IAR 317 Airfox from Romania, pictured at Paris 1985* (J. M. de Casteja).

The helicopter has been developed as a direct result of the United Nations arms embargo and to provide a strengthening of the local technology base. In March 1981, a contract for the design and manufacturing was signed with Armscor and the helicopter was first rolled out in February 1984 and flight tested a year later. According to the South Africans, the Alpha is manufactured of metal semi-monocoque and composite components with a welded pipe centre section, powered by a gas turbine engine (possibly the Turbomeca Astazou) and featuring a non-retractable undercarriage.

The GAI cannon can be moved through +10° to −60° (elevation) and +120° to −120° (azimuth), with a magazine of 1,000 rounds and a rate of fire of 600 rpm. It is possible that a larger helicopter based on the Puma design will be developed shortly.

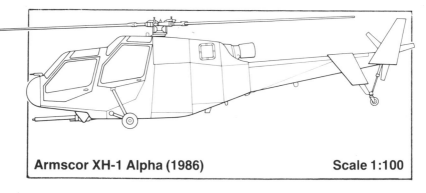

Armscor XH-1 Alpha (1986)　　　　　　　　**Scale 1:100**

IAR 317 Airfox

Details as for SE 3160 except: **Engine** 1 × Turbomeca Artouste IIIB 562 shp (derated from 870 shp); **Crew** 1 pilot, 1 co-pilot/gunner; **Passengers** 0; **Max take-off weight** 2,200 kg (4,850 lb); **Payload** 1,050 kg (2,315 kg); **Empty weight** 1,150 kg (2,535 lb); **Length** 9.8 m (32.15 ft); **Max speed** 119 kt (220 km/h); **Max cruise speed** 108 kt (200 km/h); **Service ceiling** 5,950 m (19,520 ft); **Rate of climb** N A; **HIGE** as ceiling; **HOGE** 5,600 m (18,372 ft); **Range** 283 nm (525 km); **Weapons** (anti-tank) 6 × 9M14M missiles, 2 × 7.62 mm machine guns in nose; (close-support) 4 × 57 mm rocket pods, or 4 × GMP 2 machine gun pods; (armed reconnaissance) 2 × 7.62 mm machine guns in nose and flares.

First shown at the Paris Air Show 1985, the Airfox is a direct development of the Alouette III helicopter built under licence in Roumania by the state aircraft factory at Brasov; the company also builds the Puma. The airframe is predominantly that of the Alouette III, with a modified nose section for tandem seating, with the gunner in the front. The range of weapons is impressive and the helicopter, although still in prototype form does have much potential in the Third World export market, being simple to fly and operate. The weapons suite is particularly impressive and suited to most theatres.

AEROSPATIALE SUPER FRELON SERIES

First flight 7 December 1962; **Operational** 1966

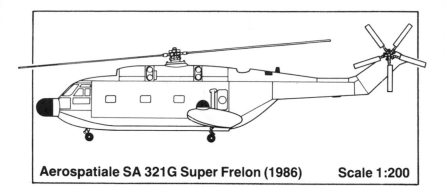

Aerospatiale SA 321G Super Frelon (1986)   **Scale 1:200**

SA 321G Super Frelon

Engines 3 × Turbomeca Turmo IIIC 1,550 shp (max cont power 1,274 shp); **Crew** 2 pilot, 1 engineer, 1 aircrewman; **Passengers** 25-27; **Max take-off weight** 13,000 kg (28,660 lb); **Payload** 6,090 kg (13,427 lb); **Empty weight** 6,863 kg (15,130 lb); **External load** 5,000 kg (11,000 lb); **Length** 20.1 m (66.1 ft); **Width** 6.2 m (17.1 ft); **Rotor diameter** 18.9 m (62 ft); **Height** 6.7 m (21.9 ft); **Max speed** 148 kt (275 km/h); **Max cruise speed** 134 kt (248 km/h); **Service ceiling** 3,100 m (10,000 ft); **Rate of climb** 5 m/sec (985 ft/min); **HIGE** 1,950 m (6,400 ft); **HOGE** N A; **Range** 443 nm (820 km); **Weapons** 7.62 mm GPMG (provision for torpedoes removed)

SA 321H Super Frelon

Planned versions for French Air Force and Army; abandoned

SA 321J Super Frelon

Utility version.

SA 321JA Super Frelon

Utility version for People's Republic of China

SA 321K Super Frelon

Assault troop carrier for Israel

SA 321L Super Frelon

Assault and marine helicopter for South Africa

SA 321M Super Frelon

For SAR, later converted to carry AM 39 Exocet anti-shipping missile for Libya and Iraq

No longer used for anti-submarine operations, the French Navy's Super Frelon helicopters are used for troop transport (Aerospatiale).

Harbin Z-8
The newly revealed Chinese-built version with new engines

Until the first flight of the EH 101, the Super Frelon was the largest production helicopter manufactured in Europe and it served for many years as the medium shipborne anti-submarine warfare helicopter of the French Navy. In the early 1980s, with the arrival of the destroyer embarked Lynx and the aircraft carrier space required for the new Super Etendard air groups, the Super Frelons were brought ashore to operate in the commando support, logistical re-supply and assault roles.

The Super Frelon was the first European helicopter designed with a boat-shaped hull for amphibious operations, although for good reasons of corrosion prevention, such operations were rarely carried out.

France exported the helicopter to the People's Republic of China for supporting the space programme and for re-supply operations with support ships. In South Africa, the helicopter was used for a troop transport but even with three engines, the power-weight ratio was not adequate for high-hot operations, so the helicopters are now used for SAR and maritime surveillance. Libya and Iraq originally acquired their SA 321 fleets for SAR and trooping but both nations have armed their helicopters with the Aerospatiale Exocet sea-skimming missile.

The most publicized use of the Super Frelon has been by the

Israeli Defence Force in operations against Egyptian positions in the Six Day War and later when the helicopters were used to transport a commando assault against a Red Sea radar station which culminated in the complete installation being brought back to Israel. In all one hundred had been built when production stopped in 1983.

AEROSPATIALE PUMA SERIES

First flight April 15 1965; **Operational** 1969

SA 330B Puma

Production version for the French Army, powered by 2 × Turbomeca Turmo IIIC engines

SA 330C Puma

Export version, powered by Turmo IIIC

SA 330E Puma

Co-produced version for Royal Air Force, first flight 1970

SA 330H Puma

Version for French Army and export

SA 330L Puma

Engines 2 × Turbomeca Turmo IVC 1,494 shp (max cont power 1,262

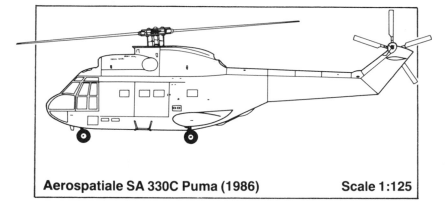

Aerospatiale SA 330C Puma (1986)　　　　　**Scale 1:125**

Exercising with infantry, this SA 330 Puma is operated by the French ALAT (Army Light Aviation); note the intake filters (Paul Beaver).

shp); **Crew** 1-2 pilots, 1 aircrewman; **Passengers** 20-22; **Max take-off weight** 7,400 kg (16,315 lb); **Payload** 3,759 kg (8,288 lb); **Empty weight** 3,615 kg (7,970 lb); **External load** 3,500 kg (7,715 lb); **Length** 14.82 m (48.62 ft); **Width** 3.62 m (11.87 ft); **Rotor diameter** 15.1 m (49.8 ft); **Height** 5.14 m (16.9 ft); **Max speed** 142 kt (263 km/h); **Max cruise speed** 139 kt (258 km/h); **Service ceiling** 4,800 m (15,750 ft); **Rate of climb** 6.1 m/sec (1,200 ft/min); **HIGE** 2,300 m (7,545 ft); **HOGE** 1,700 m (5,580 ft); **Range** 550 km (297 nm); **Weapons** door-mounted 7.62 mm GPMG (can carry 20 mm cannon or rockets)

IAR 330 Puma
Licence-produced in Roumania and still in production

NSA 330 Puma
Licence-produced in Indonesia, production has ceased

As a result of the French Army's experience with helicopters in the Algerian colonial war, a requirement was issued in 1962 for a light-medium troop support helicopter, capable of all-weather operations. The helicopter was selected by the French military in 1965 and by the UK Royal Air Force in 1967; in 1969, the Puma became part of the Anglo-French helicopter agreement (which also included co-production of the Gazelle and Lynx). The first French production helicopter flew in September 1968 and the first UK-built airframe flew in November 1970.

The helicopter was an export success being delivered to Abu Dhabi, Algeria, Argentina, Belgium, Brazil, Chile, Chad, Congo, Ecuador, Ethiopia, Gabon, Guinea Rep., Indonesia, Iraq, Ivory Coast, Kenya, Kuwait, Lebanon, Malawi, Mexico, Morocco, Nepal, Nigeria, Pakistan, Portugal, Roumania, Senegambia, South Africa, Spain, Sudan, Togo and Zaire.

The Puma has seen action in southern Africa with South African, Rhodesian and Portugese forces, being used daily in the 'operational area' in SWA/Namibia and Angola. A Puma was the first casualty of the Falklands conflict, being destroyed on South Georgia, and Argentine Pumas were active in the Falklands, one coastguard machine was destroyed at Port Stanley (its hulk was returned to Britain), five other army SA 330Ls were destroyed during the fighting.

Recent trials have been carried out by the Portugese for air-to-air refuelling using a trailing fuel line which plugs into the tanker aircraft; other developments include trainable door-gun and cannon mountings as well as specialist equipment for Antarctic use by Argentina and South Africa. So successful has the type been that it is destined to remain in service for many years.

AEROSPATIALE GAZELLE SERIES

First flight 7 April 1967; **Operational** 1972

SA 341B Gazelle
Production version for the British Army (Gazelle AH 1)

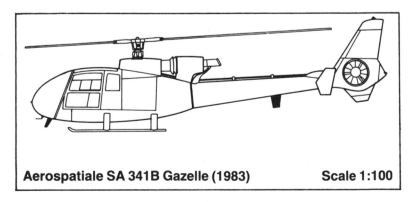

Aerospatiale SA 341B Gazelle (1983)   **Scale 1:100**

Made under licence in Yugoslavia, the SOKO 342 is armed with Soviet-made anti-tank missiles and a French sight (Aerospatiale).

SA 341C Gazelle
Production version for the Royal Navy (Gazelle HT 2)

SA 341D Gazelle
Production version for the RAF (Gazelle HT 3)

SA 341E Gazelle
Production version for the RAF (Gazelle HCC 4)

SA 341F Gazelle
Production version for the French Army

SA 341H Gazelle
Built under licence by SOKO in Yugoslavia

SA 342K Gazelle
Export hot/high version

SA 342L Gazelle
Engine 1 × Turbomeca Astazou XIVH 592 shp; **Crew** 1-2 pilots; **Passengers** 3-4; **Max take-off weight** 1,900 kg (4,190 lb); **Payload** 918 kg (2,026 lb); **Empty weight** 975 kg (2,149 lb); **External load** 700 kg (1,540 lb); **Length** 9.53 m (31.3 ft); **Width** 2.01 m (6.6 ft); **Rotor**

diameter 10.5 m (34.5 ft); **Height** 3.18 m (10.45 ft); **Max speed** 167 kt (310 km/h); **Max cruise speed** 142 kt (264 km/h); **Service ceiling** 4,300 m (14,105 ft); **Rate of climb** 8.5 m/sec (1,675 ft/min); **HIGE** 3,650 m (11,970 ft); **HOGE** 2,875 m (9,430 ft); **Range** 755 km (407 nm); **Weapons** (anti-tank): 4 × HOT/AT-3 Sagger, 1 × 20 mm Giat cannon; (close support) 1 × 20 mm cannon, rocket launchers, 2 × 7.62 mm GPMG.

SA 342LE Gazelle
Licence-produced in Egypt and by SOKO

SA 342M Gazelle
Production version for French Army with Astazou XIVM

Designed to be a successor to the Alouette II, the Gazelle is a widely used battlefield observation and liaison helicopter which has seen action in the Falkland Islands, Lebanon and North Africa. More than twenty armed forces operate the helicopter and production has been carried out in France, UK (Westland), Yugoslavia (SOKO) and Egypt (Arab-British); the helicopter remains in production in all except Britain.

Using a main rotor system jointly developed with MBB in Federal Germany and with the fenestron (shrouded) tail rotor system, the Gazelle is an agile and well-balanced helicopter. In the pure observation role, it is fitted with direct view or thermal imaging optics, but it can be used with machine, cannon, rocket or guided missile armament. Both the French and Syrian armies have used the helicopter in an anti-tank role with the Euromissile HOT system, whilst the Moroccan forces have deployed the helicopter with 20 mm cannon and missiles during combat in the Sahara conflict against the Polisario.

The SA 341 version was uprated for hot/high operations and designated the SA 342 in 1973; some versions are fitted with particle separators to prevent dust/sand penetration to the engine. In anti-terrorist situations, IR shields can be fitted and there is provision for a weapons/stores boom.

AEROSPATIALE DAUPHIN SERIES

First flight 2 June 1972; **Operational** 1975

Carrying four AS 15TT anti-shipping missiles, the SA 365F Dauphin 2 has been delivered to the Saudi Arabian Navy (Aerospatiale).

SA 361H Dauphin
Was a private venture for multi-role applications

SA 365C Dauphin 2
Operated by the Royal Hong Kong Auxiliary Air Force

SA 365F Naval Dauphin 2
Engines 2 × Turbomeca Arriel 520M 700 shp (max cont power 627 shp); **Crew** 2 pilots, 1 crewman; **Passengers** up to 9; **Max take-off weight** 3,900 kg (8,000 lb); **Payload** 1,370 kg (3,023 lb); **Empty weight** 2,530 kg (5,577 lb); **External load** 1,700 kg (3,748 lb); **Length** 12.11 m (39.7 ft); **Width** 3.21 m (10.5 ft); **Rotor diameter** 11.9 m (39.1 ft); **Height** 3.99 m (13.1 ft); **Max speed** 165 kt (306 km/h); **Max cruise speed** 140 kt (260 km/h); **Service ceiling** 4,575 m (15,000 ft); **Rate of climb** 7.7 m/sec (1,515 ft/min); **HIGE** 2,550 m (8,365 ft); **HOGE** 1,750 m (5,740 ft); **Range** 758 km (410 nm); **Weapons** (ASW) 1 × MAD + 2 × Mk 46 torpedo or 1 × dipping sonar + 1 × torpedo; (ASV) 4 × AS 15TT missiles

SA 365M Dauphin 2
The battlefield version (see Panther)

SA 365N Dauphin 2
The communications/liaison/VIP version

SA 365 Panther
A light multi-mission helicopter

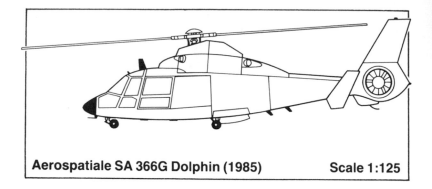

Aerospatiale SA 366G Dolphin (1985)   **Scale 1:125**

SA 366G Dolphin
The US Coast Guard version with Avco-Lycoming LTS 101-750 engines and an advanced Collins mission management system

Harbin Z-9
The Chinese-built version

Development of the Dauphin series began in the early 1970s with a single Astazou-engined version but the helicopter was rapidly developed for the potential large military market with two engines. The Naval Dauphin has been sold to the Saudi Arabian naval air arm for anti-ship and anti-submarine warfare roles. The helicopter is equipped with the TRT Omega ORB 32 radar.

In 1980, China signed an agreement to produce the SA 365N for para-military operations in the People's Republic and the US government made the SA 366G (American-engined version) its first foreign helicopter purchase within months. The Dolphin version is predominantly US-equipped and entered Coast Guard service in 1985; it has also been purchased by Israel.

In April 1986, Aerospatiale announced that it had uprated the Dauphin 2 into the Panther multi-mission helicopter with an all-up weight of 4,100 kg (9,040 lb) for tactical transport (10 commandoes), fire support (cannon and rockets), anti-tank (eight HOT missiles and day/night sight) and anti-helicopter warfare (armed with eight Matra Mistral missiles and two 20 mm cannon). Powered by two Turbomeca TM 333-1M engines, the helicopter has an endurance of 4 hours and a range of 750 km (405 nm). The helicopter has a number of secondary roles, including acting as a command post, SAR, reconnaissance, external load carrier and air ambulance. According to the manufacturer, the Panther is discreet and has a low infra-red signature, as well as a reduced radar signature over the SA 365N. As with all the SA 365 series, the helicopter has a large amount of composite material used in its construction and is fitted with crash-resistant fuel tanks.

AEROSPATIALE SUPER PUMA SERIES

First flight 5 September 1977; **Operational** 1981

AS 332B Super Puma

Engines 2 × Turbomeca Makila 1A 1,661 shp (max cont power 1,514 shp); **Crew** 1-2 pilots, 1 aircrewman; **Passengers** 20-21; **Max take-off weight** 8,350 kg (18,410 lb); **Payload** 4,234 kg (9,335 lb); **Empty weight** 4,100 kg (9,040 lb); **External load** 4,500 kg (9,920 lb); **Length** 15.48 m (50.8 ft); **Width** 3.79 m (12.43 ft); **Rotor diameter** 15.6 m (51.1 ft); **Height** 4.6 m (15.1 ft); **Max speed** 160 kt (296 km/h); **Max cruise speed** 151 kt (279 km/h); **Service ceiling** 4,600 m (15,088 ft); **Rate of climb** 8.8 m/sec (1,732 ft/min); **HIGE** 2,700 m (8,856 ft); **HOGE** 2,100 m (6,888 ft); **Range** 620 km (335 nm); **Weapons** (close support) 20 mm cannon, rockets or missiles; generally unarmed. Uprated version is B1.

AS 332F Super Puma

The naval version with optional weapons (ASV) 2 × AM 39 Exocet, or 4 × AS 15TT; (ASW) 1 × dipping sonar + 2 × Mk 46 torpedoes, or sonobouys and up to 4 × Murene torpedoes

AS 332M Super Puma

The stretched version at length 16.25 m (53.31 ft)

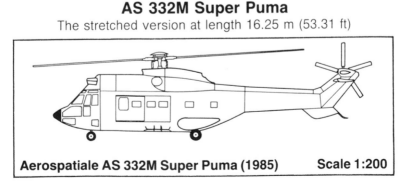

Aerospatiale AS 332M Super Puma (1985)   **Scale 1:200**

Launching an Exocet anti-ship missile, the AS 332F Super Puma has yet to attract orders for squadron service with any navy (SNIAS).

NAS 322 Super Puma

Built under licence by IPTN Nurtanio in Indonesia for that nation's armed forces, including naval use

The primary design rationale behind the Super Puma was an improved performance assault transport to follow the Puma in battlefield helicopter operations. Aerospatiale also capitalized on the uprating to provide a varied weapons and equipment fit, including the provision of Exocet for the AS 332F, which version is thought to have been delivered to Abu Dhabi.

Local assembly of the helicopter has been licenced in Indonesia, where IPTN Nurtanio has a production line at Bandung and in Singapore where the first locally Singapore Aircraft Industries-assembled AS 332Ms entered service in 1986.

Search and rescue customers have included the Spanish Air Force (ten) and Singapore, but the majority of the recent sales have been for battlefield support tasks, including the re-equipment of the Argentine Army Aviation (Ejercito) and the winning of the competition in Spain (against the advice of the army aviation or

FAMET) for more than twenty. Other customers include Abu Dhabi, Chile, Kuwait, Oman and the French government for work in Micronesia. It is expected that a large order for the French ALAT (army light aviation) will be announced soon.

The naval version has not sold as well as expected, with only two reported orders by mid-1986 (to Kuwait and Brazil) and the continued use of the helicopter by the Indonesian armed forces. A fierce competition was held with Westland for an Indian order and the helicopter is in the running for the Canadian Sea King replacement programme.

In the early 1980s, Aerospatiale offered a version of the Super Puma to the UK Royal Air Force as the Wessex/Puma replacement under a programme called AST 404; a decision was shelved in 1985 and is awaiting a full review of British support helicopter operations.

AEROSPATIALE ECUREUIL SERIES

AS 350B Ecureuil
The original liaison helicopter model; in 1985 it was uprated to B1 standards

AS 350L Ecureuil
The basic military version which has now been superceded

Built under licence in Brazil, the HB 350B is used for liaison duties aboard Brazil's aircraft carrier, Minas Gerais (Brazilian Navy).

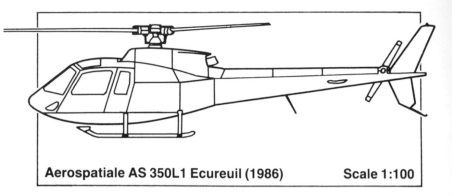

Aerospatiale AS 350L1 Ecureuil (1986)   **Scale 1:100**

AS 350L1 Ecureuil

Engine 1 × Turbomeca Arriel 1D 684 shp (max cont power 603 shp); **Crew** 1-2 pilots; **Passengers** 4-5; **Max take-off weight** 2,150 kg (4,740 lb); **Payload** 876 kg (1,932 lb); **Empty weight** 1,108 kg (2,443 lb); **External load** 907 kg (2,000 lb); **Length** 10.9 m (35.9 ft); **Width** 2.53 m (8.3 ft); **Rotor diameter** 10.7 m (35.1 ft); **Height** 3.14 m (10.3 ft); **Max speed** 147 kt (272 km/h); **Cruise speed** 124 kt (230 km/h); **Service ceiling** 4,500 m (14,760 ft); **Rate of climb** 7.5 m/sec (1,500 ft/min); **HIGE** 2,870 m (9,400 ft); **HOGE** 1,920 m (6,300 ft); **Range** 655 km (354 nm); **Weapons** 1 × 20 mm Giat cannon + rockets, or 2 × cannon, or machine guns

Helibras HB 350B

The Brazilian-built version called the Esquilo

AS 355F Ecureuil 2

The basic twin-engined version; uprated to F1 in 1985

AS 355M1 Ecureuil

The basic military twin-engined version which has now been superceded

AS 355M2 Ecureuil 2

Engines 2 × Allison 250-C20F 420 shp; **Crew** 2 pilots; **Passengers** 3; **Max take-off weight** 2,540 kg (5,600 lb); **Payload** 1,180 kg (2,600 lb); **Empty weight** 1,360 kg (2,998 lb); **External load** 1,134 kg (2,500 lb); **Length, Width, Rotor diameter and Height** as AS 350L1; **Max speed** 150 kt (278 km/h); **Max cruise speed** 121 kt (224 km/h); **Service ceiling** 3,400 m (11,150 ft); **Rate of climb** 6.5 m/sec (1,280 ft/min); **HIGE** 1,800

m (5,900 ft); **HOGE** 1,350 m (4,425 ft); **Range** 380 nm (703 km);
Weapons (anti-tank) 4/6 TOW or HOT wire-guided missiles; (close
support) combination of 70 mm rocket pods, 20, 12.7 or 7.62 mm gun
pods; (self-defence) Matra Misral missiles

AS 355M Ecureuil 2

Powered by 2 × Turbomeca TM 319 engines 443 shp for the
French Air Force

At present, Aerospatiale is finding that procurement of the Ecureuil
(Squirrel) family is slower than expected, mainly because the
major projected customers already operate Aerospatiale types
which are still offering good service. Nevertheless, with the
introduction of the AS 350L1 model in 1985, the French helicopter
industry believes that it has an excellent cost-effective military
helicopter for tasks ranging from simple liaison operations to light
support and ground attack, when mounting the Giat 20 mm cannon
and/or the Thomson Brandt or Forges de Zeebrugge rocket
systems.

The major customer for some 50 AS 355M is the French Air
Force, which is re-engining the helicopter with the Turbomeca TM
319 and specifying fully compatible cockpits for night vision goggle
operations. The helicopters will be used for liaison and special
transport tasks for the Force de Frappe (strategic weapon
organization). Although not specified by France, the manufacturer
can provide the Ecureuil 2 with pylons for Euromissile HOT
anti-tank missiles as well as sub-munition rocket launchers and
cannon.

By mid-1986, interest had been shown by a number of nations
and orders placed by the Royal Australian Air Force and Navy, the
Singapore Air Force and the armed forces of Botswana, Central
African Republic, Swaziland, Malawi, Tunisia and Djibouti. Future
military and police orders are expected, especially for the
proposed AS 350Z helicopter which features the Gazelle-type
fenestron shrouded tail rotor.

AGUSTA

AGUSTA A 109 SERIES

First flight 4 August 1971; **Operational** 1976

A 109A Hirundo

Engines 2 × Allison 250-C20B 420 shp (max cont power 420 shp); **Crew** 1-2 pilots; **Passengers** 6-7; **Max take-off weight** 2,600 kg (5,732 lb); **Payload** 1,119 kg (2,467 lb); **Empty weight** 1,459 kg (3,216 lb); **External load** 907 kg (2,000 lb); **Length** 10.7 m (35.12 ft); **Width** 2.88 m (9.4 ft); **Rotor diameter** 11 m (36.1 ft); **Height** 3.3 m (10.9 ft); **Max speed** 168 kt (311 km/h); **Max cruise speed** 147 kt (272 km/h); **Service ceiling** 4,968 m (16,300 ft); **Rate of climb** 8.2 m/sec (1,620 ft/min); **HIGE** 2,987 m (9,800 ft); **HOGE** 2,042 m (6,700 ft); **Range** 565 km (305 nm); **Weapons** (anti-tank) 4 × TOW; (close support) 2 × 70 mm rocket pods and/or cannon or 12.7 mm door-mounted gun

A 109A Mk II
The updated version available from September 1981

A 109CSG
The dedicated coastguard and para-military version

A 109 Naval
Designed for shipborne or shore use

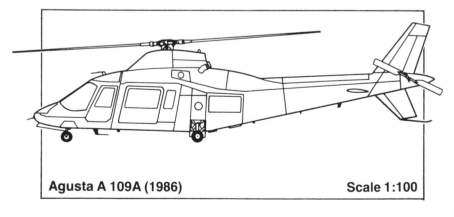

Agusta A 109A (1986)   **Scale 1:100**

Agusta's first successful helicopter is the A 109, seen here in Italian ALE colours with TOW missiles on launchers (Agusta).

A 109K
The Turbomeca Arriel 723 shp powered, fixed undercarriage version

Agusta, the state-owned helicopter manufacturer in Italy designed the A 109 in the mid-1960s as a modern turbine-engined helicopter with high speed and agility. The A 109A Hirundo is suitable for a number of tasks including aerial scouting, light attack/close support, command and control, utility/liaison and electronic warfare. The rear cabin can accommodate six troops with the stick commander flying in the cockpit's left-hand seat alongside the pilot.

To prove the A 129 Mongoose concept, a small batch of A 109A helicopters were purchased by the Italian ALE (Army Light Aviation) to be fitted with the Hughes Aircraft M65 chin-mounted sight and four TOW wire-guided anti-tank missiles. In addition, the helicopter is capable of carrying rocket and gun pods.

The A 109 Naval could be fitted with a towed magnetic anomaly detector and two Motorfides/Whitehead A 244/S lightweight torpedoes with an endurance of nearly 2 hours at 80 kt (150 km/h). For anti-shipping operations, the A 109 could be fitted with the Nord AS 12, a stabilized sight and a lightweight search radar. At sea or over the battlefield the helicopter also makes an interesting and effective electronic warfare helicopter and is believed to be in service with the Italian Army for such tasks.

Besides Italian service, the A 109 has been purchased by Argentina, Iraq, Libya and Venezuela. In 1983, it was decided to purchase two A 109A Mk II helicopters for the British Army for special operations, joining two captured Argentine Hirundoes for use by the Special Air Service. The A 109K version was said to have been originally designed with French engines to overcome an American ban on the export of any military goods to Libya, because the helicopters' engines are manufactured in the United States. It is now thought that the K model is ideally suited to hot and high desert conditions such as those found in the Middle East, especially Saudi Arabia, a nation which has just formed an army aviation corps.

AGUSTA A 129 SERIES

First flight 15 September 1983; **Operational** 1987

A 129 Mangusta

Engines 2 × Rolls-Royce Mk 1004 881 shp (max cont power 825); **Crew** 1 pilot, 1 co-pilot/gunner; **Passengers** 0; **Max take-off weight** 3,800 kg (8,377 lb); **Payload** 1,738 kg (3,832 lb); **Empty weight** 2,062 kg (4,545 lb); **External load** 1,200 kg (2,645 lb); **Length** 12.31 m (40.4 ft); **Width** 3.6 m (11.8 ft); **Rotor diameter** 11.9 m (39.04 ft); **Height** 3.35 m (11 ft); **Max speed** 150 kt (278 km/h); **Max cruise speed** 135 kt (250 km/h); **Service ceiling** 5,502 m (18,050 ft); **Rate of climb** 10 m/sec (1,968 ft/min); **HIGE** 3,749 m (12,300 ft); **HOGE** 2,999 m (9,840 ft); **Range** 741 km (400 nm); **Weapons** (anti-tank 8 × TOW/HOT or 6 × Hellfire + 2 × 70 mm rocket pods; (close support) 4 × gun pods or 4 × 70 mm rocket pods; (anti-helicopter) 8 × Stinger or Mistral and 1 × 12.7 mm gun turret

Agusta A 129 Mangusta (1986)   **Scale 1:125**

The first dedicated light attack helicopter to fly in Europe, the Agusta A 129 Mangusta will be the basis of a multi-national programme.

A 129 Mk 2
Initially proposed variant for the British Army

A 129 Tonal
The four nation Light Attack Helicopter concept

A 129 Utility/LSH
Possible light support helicopter derivative

A 129 Naval
A proposed attack version capable of shipborne operations carrying a range of anti-shipping missiles

The Mangusta is the first of the European dedicated attack/anti-tank helicopters to fly and it entered service with the Italian ALE (Army Light Aviation) in 1987. Since its first flight in 1983, it has impressed observers by its low noise, low canopy glint and overall compactness. Agusta has designed the helicopter with a very small cross section, minimum visual detection, a low infra-red signature and reduced exposure for the two-man crew.

The initial variant for the Italian Army is powered by British engines and uses the new Martin Baker crashworthy helicopter seat, in addition to which the integrated multiplex avionics system (navigation, mission management, fire control and systems monitoring) is produced jointly by Agusta OMI and the Harris Corporation of Florida. The first helicopters will be armed with the Hughes Aircraft TOW system, using a chin-mounted direct view optical sight and Ferranti Honeywell Forward Looking Infra-Red (FLIR), but later helicopters are expected to be fitted with a mast-mounted sighting system with laser designation for the Rockwell Hellfire missiles. The TOW-armed version has been ordered by Abu Dhabi.

In 1984 it was revealed that the British Army was studying the A 129 to fulfil the role of its Light Attack Helicopter planned for the 1995-97 period to replace the Gazelle and Lynx/TOW with British Army of the Rhine. In 1986, the four governments of Italy, UK, Netherlands and Spain signed a memorandum of understanding to develop the Tonal, an advanced version of the A 129. This helicopter design study will be completed in 1989, but features such as the Rolls-Royce/Turbomeca RTM 322 engine, an advanced 'glass' cockpit, the European Trigat missile system and a Lucas Aerospace 12.7 mm gun turret could be fitted.

Amongst the new technology being developed for the complete A 129 programme is the use of composite materials, made from apoxy-graphite and other blends, including the main rotor system's blades and hub. Composite materials have a longer life and are more 'survivable' in combat than traditional metals. The helicopter has also been designed for low maintenance and has built-in test equipment to detect faults before they become critical to the helicopter's performance.

AGUSTA AB 212/AB 412 SERIES

First flight 1972; Operational 1977

AB 212ASW

Engines 2 × Pratt & Whitney of Canada PT6T-6 Twin Pac 1,875 shp (max cont power 1,130 shp); **Crew** 3-4; **Passengers** 1 (6-7 in trooping role); **Max take-off weight** 5,070 kg (11,176 lb); **Payload** 1,650 kg (3,636 lb); **Empty weight** 3,420 kg (7,540 lb); **External load** 2,270 kg (5,000 lb); **Length** 14.02 m (46 ft); **Width** 4.17 m (13.68 ft); **Rotor diameter** 14.63 m (48 ft); **Height** 4.4 m (14.43 ft); **Max speed** 130 kt (240 km/h); **Max cruise speed** 106 kt (196 km/h); **Service ceiling** 4,330 m (14,200 ft); **Rate of climb** 6.6 m/sec (1,300 ft/min); **HIGE** 3,200 m (10,500 ft); **HOGE** 396 m (1,300 ft); **Range** 426 km (230 nm); **Weapons** (anti-submarine) 2

Operating from frigates and destroyers, the AB 212ASW is a potent anti-submarine and anti-ship helicopter in Italian naval service.

× Mk 46 torpedoes with AQS-13B sonar or ASQ-81 MAD; (anti-ship) 2 × AS 12 or Marte missiles with ARI 5955 radar, or 4 × Sea Skua with Sea Spray radar; (electronic warfare) various ESM and ECM systems

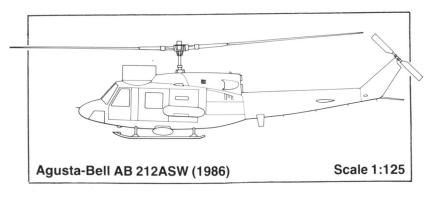

Agusta-Bell AB 212ASW (1986)   **Scale 1:125**

AB 412 Griffon

Engine as AB 212ASW; **Crew** 2-3; **Passengers** up to 15; **Max take-off weight** 5,261 kg (11,600 lb); **Payload** 2,293 kg (5,057 lb); **Empty weight** 2,841 kg (6,263 lb); **External load** 1,814 kg (4,000 lb); **Length** 12.7 m (41.7 ft); **Width** 2.6 m (8.5 ft); **Rotor diameter** 14.02 m (46 ft); **Height** 3.29 m (10.8 ft); **Max speed** 140 kt (259 km/h); **Max cruise speed** 122 kt (226 km/h); **Service ceiling** 4,330 m (14,200 ft); **Rate of climb** 6.7 m/sec (1,320 ft/min); **HIGE** 3,350 m (11,000 ft); **HOGE** 610 m (2,000 ft); **Range** 227 nm (420 km); **Weapons** (anti-tank) 4-8 TOW missiles; (close support) 19 × 70 mm rockets in pods; (tactical) machine gun and cannon pods

Built using a licence from Bell Helicopter Textron, the Agusta-Bell 212ASW is a direct development on the now obsolete AB 204 single-engined anti-submarine helicopter which carried two Mk 44 lightweight torpedoes and was operated by the Italian and Spanish navies. The AB 212ASW is the standard small ship helicopter in the ASW and ASVW roles for the Italian, Spanish, Turkish, Peruvian and Venezuelan navies.

The standard crew configuration is a pilot, co-pilot, sonar operator and radar operator/tactical commander for the anti-submarine role, although if the helicopter is fitted a magnetic anomaly detector (MAD) the sonar operator is not carried. For rescue operations, up to seven survivors could be carried depending on fuel load and for vertrep (vertical replenishment) operations can be carried out for nearly 2 hours; EW operations can have 5 hours.

As a direct result of the licence-built AB 212 troop transport (see Bell 212 series), Agusta developed the four-bladed Griffon helicopter for the tactical transport helicopter market. It first flew in August 1982 and the first examples were delivered to the Italian Army Aviation (ALE) in 1986. The helicopter has since been ordered in some numbers by African nations, particularly Zimbabwe and Lesotho, but no major market has been found for the helicopter.

As a tactical transport and multi-role helicopter, the Griffon is credited with good performance in hot/high conditions and can readily carry supporting weapons when used in the assault role. Besides weapons, the helicopter carries ESM and ECM systems, dependent upon the customer's needs and abilities. A special performance version is being developed.

BELL HELICOPTER TEXTRON

BELL 47 SERIES

First flight 8 December 1945; **Operational** 1946

H-13 Sioux
Built for the US armed forces in considerable numbers

H-13D
A variant used for casualty evacuation in the Korean War

H-13H
The US Air Force version

H-13J
The first US Presidential version

OH-13 Sioux
The observation version, exported in the H variant

Shown here in Brazilian Air Force markings, the Bell H-13/47 Sioux series is still in widespread but decreasing service (Brazilian AF).

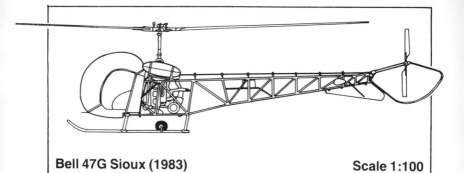

Bell 47G Sioux (1983)   **Scale 1:100**

TH-13L/M/N Sioux
These were the training versions

TH-13T
This was the instrument training version

UH-13 Sioux
The utility version

HTL-3
The US naval version for student training

47G Sioux AH 1
This was the Westland-built version for the British Army

47G Sioux HT 2
The training version

Agusta-Bell 47J-3
The Italian version with Mk 44 lightweight torpedo

H-13H Sioux
Engine 1 × Lycoming VO-435 200 hp piston; **Crew** 1 pilot; **Passengers** 2; **Max take-off weight** 1,112 kg (2,450 kg); **Payload** 479 kg (1,057 lb); **Empty weight** 710 kg (1,564 lb); **External load** 454 kg (1,000 lb); **Length** 9.63 m (31.6 ft); **Width** 2.5 m (8.3 ft); **Rotor diameter** 11.3 m

(37.1 ft); **Height** 2.9 m (9.5 ft); **Max speed** 87 kt (161 km/h); **Max cruise speed** 74 kt (137 km/h); **Service ceiling** 4,023 m (13,200 ft); **Rate of climb** 3.6 m/sec (700 ft/min); **HIGE** 5,060 m (16,600 ft); **HOGE** 3,750 m (12,300 ft); **Range** 261 nm (483 km); **Weapons** generally unarmed but could carry 7.62 mm machine gun

The first really successful commercial helicopter was modified for service use in 1946 when it joined the US Navy as the HTL-2; the US Army evaluation model was the YR-13, powered by a Franklin engine and having enclosed tailboom. As the H-13, the Bell Model 47 really made its mark during the Korean War (1950-53) acting as a casualty evacuation helicopter for the United Nations forces as immortalized in the MASH series on television. The helicopter was flown by a single pilot in his perspex bubble, with two stretcher paniers alongside on the skids. Later H-13s were fitted with floats.

The H-13 was operated by the French ALAT in the Algerian war and later took part in many conflicts, notably with the British Army and Royal Marines in Borneo during the confrontation with Indonesia. In a more peaceful role, the Bell 47 has acted as the basic instrument and advanced training helicopter for the armed forces of the world being in service, at one time or another with over thirty nations. It remains in service with several major armed services, including the Italian ALE (licence-built variants from Agusta) and the Japanese Self-Defence Forces (licence-built by Kawasaki) modified to the KH-4 a four-seat light utility helicopter derived from the 47G-3 for the JGSDF (army).

The British armed forced selected the type as the Westland Sioux in the early 1960s, using it for forward reconnaissance and liaison with various air troops where apart from Aden and Borneo, it gave sterling service in Northern Ireland until replaced by the Gazelle. The last Bell and Agusta-built helicopters were delivered in 1973 but there is a considerable used market for both civil and military operators.

BELL 204/205 SERIES

First flight 22 October 1956 (204); 16 August 1961 (205); **Operational** 1959 (204); 1963 (205)

HU-1A Iroquois
The initial production variant

Operating in support of Swedish ground troops, the venerable AB 204 (an Italian-built Huey) is overdue for replacement (FLC/Sjögren).

HU-1B Iroquois/UH-1B from 1962

Engine 1 × Lycoming T53-L-11 1,100 shp; **Crew** 2 pilots; **Passengers** 7; **Max take-off weight** 3,856 kg (8,500 lb); **Payload** 1,769 kg (3,900 lb); **Empty weight** 2,087 kg (4,600 lb); **External load** 1,814 kg (4,000 lb); **Length** 12.3 m (40.42 ft); **Width** 2.6 m (8.6 ft); **Rotor diameter** 13.4 m (44 ft); **Height** 4.42 m (14.5 ft); **Max speed** 129 kt (238 km/h); **Max cruise speed** 104 kt (193 km/h); **Service ceiling** 3,505 m (11,500 ft); **Rate of climb** 7.5 m/sec (1,418 ft/min); **HIGE** 3,231 m (10,600 ft); **HOGE** 3,048 m (10,000 ft); **Range** 332 nm (615 km); **Weapons** (close-support) 2 × 12.7 mm guns, 2 × 40 mm grenade launchers; (trooping) 12.7 mm door guns only

UH-1C Huey

Modified rotor version

UH-1E Huey

Armed version for the US Marine Corps

UH-1F Huey

Combat rescue version for the US Air Force; TH-1F is a trainer

A Bell UH-1F search and rescue helicopter is just one of the many Huey variants; these are the colours of the US Air Force (US DoD).

HH-1K Huey
Combat rescue version for the US Navy

UH-1L Huey
US Navy utility version; TH-1L is trainer

UH-1M Huey
More powerful C version

UH-1P Huey
All-weather version of F model

Agusta AB204B
The Italian-built version with the Rolls-Royce Gnome engine

Fuji UH-1B
Built under licence in Japan

UH-1D Huey
Enlarged version, designated Model 205

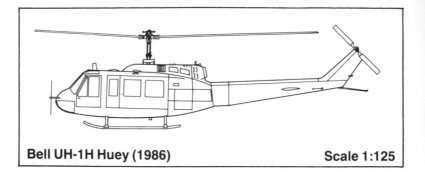

Bell UH-1H Huey (1986)　　　　　　　　**Scale 1:125**

UH-1H Huey

Engine 1 × Lycoming T53-L-13B 1,400 shp (max cont power 1,250 shp); **Crew** 1-3; **Passengers** 11-13; **Max take-off weight** 4,309 kg (9,500 lb); **Payload** 2,006 kg (4,422 lb); **Empty weight** 2,303 kg (5,078 lb); **External load** 2,269 kg (5,000 lb); **Length** 12.4 m (40.6 ft); **Width** 2.62 m (8.6 ft); **Rotor diameter** 14.63 m (48 ft); **Height** 4.42 m (14.5 ft); **Max speed** 128 kt (237 km/h); **Max cruise speed** 110 kt (204 km/h); **Service ceiling** 3,871 m (12,700 ft); **Rate of climb** 8.1 m/sec (1,600 ft/min); **HIGE** 3,170 m (10,400 ft); **HOGE** 1,830 m (6,004 ft); **Range** 270 nm (500 km); **Weapons** various guns and rocket pods (especially in Vietnam)

EH-1H Quick Fix
The electronic warfare version

HH-1H Huey
The USAF rescue version

CH-118
The Canadian version (formerly CUH-1H)

Agusta AB 205/AB 205A
The Italian-built variant for home and export use

AIDC 205A
The Taiwanese-built version; 118 delivered

Dornier UH-1D
Built under licence in Federal Germany; 352 delivered

The Bell 204/205 series, originally called the Iroquois but now universally known by the US forces nickname of Huey is a remarkable helicopter, with over 10,000 helicopters having been completed at various locations around the world. The helicopter did more than any other to revolutionize land warfare, especially during the 1965-72 Vietnam War, in the Arab-Israeli wars, against separatists in Sri Lanka, in the mountains of Oman, the bush of Rhodesia (now Zimbabwe) and in other para-military actions around the globe.

The Bell design was developed to fulfil a US Army requirement for casevac and general utility work born out of the Korean War but the helicopter did not enter quantity production until the US involvement in South-East Asia had developed into full-scale war. Based with the 11th Air Assault Division, the UH-1 was the vehicle in which the US armed forces developed the art of air mobility and air assault which led to air cavalry and other concepts.

Today, the US Army is still a major user of the type which will not be fully replaced until about 2000, when 2,700 will still remain on the books of the regular Army Aviation, Army National Guard and Army Reserve. In other nations, it will run on in various guises until 2010 at least. The Federal German Bundeswehr is delaying its replacement programme because there is still useful life in the design yet, especially with night vision goggle and forward looking infra-red (FLIR) equipment. In 1985, the Turkish government asked Bell to reopen the UH-1H production line for a substantial order of utility, electronic warfare and SAR helicopters. In addition, the helicopters are still sought after on the used aircraft markets of the world and seem destined to remain in front-line operations for many years to come.

The Agusta-Bell 204 has been used as a support helicopter and also as a naval helicopter with various equipment and rotor blade changes; some of the latter type were also in service with the Turkish and Peruvian navies but have been replaced with the AB 212ASW (see separate entry).

BELL 206 SERIES

First flight 10 January 1966; **Operational** 1968

206A JetRanger
The basic liaison version

206B JetRanger
This model has an improved powerplant

206L LongRanger
The stretched liaison helicopter

206L TexasRanger
The armed version of the LongRanger; few sold

OH-58A Kiowa
Engine 1 × Allison 250-C20J 420 shp (max cont power 370 shp); **Crew** 2 pilots; **Passengers** 3; **Max take-off weight** 1,451 kg (3,200 lb); **Payload** 705 kg (1,555 lb); **Empty weight** 746 kg (1,645 lb); **External load** 680 kg (1,500 lb); **Length** 9.5 m (31.2 ft); **Width** 1.95 m (6.4 ft); **Rotor diameter** 10.15 m (33.3 ft); **Height** 2.91 m (9.5 ft); **Max speed** 122 kt (226 km/h); **Max cruise speed** 115 kt (213 km/h); **Service ceiling** 4,115 m (13,500 ft); **Rate of climb** 6.4 m/sec (1,260 ft/min); **HIGE** 3,901 m (12,800 ft); **HOGE** 2,682 m (8,800 ft); **Range** 368 nm (682 km); **Weapons** 2 × 7.62 mm machine guns, 14 × 70 mm rockets

TH-57A SeaRanger
The US Navy's basic training helicopter

CH-136 Kiowa
The Canadian observation helicopter

Agusta AB 206A
The Italian-built version

CAC 206B Kiowa
The Australian-built version

TH-57B SeaRanger
The US Navy's improved primary trainer

OH-58C Kiowa
The US Army's scout and air defence helicopter

TH-57C SeaRanger
The new advanced instrument trainer

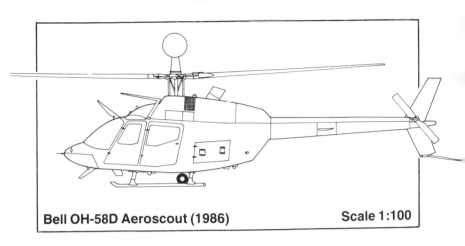

Bell OH-58D Aeroscout (1986)   **Scale 1:100**

OH-58D Aeroscout

Engine 1 × Allison 250-C30R 650 shp; **Crew** 1 pilot, 1 observer; **Passengers** 0; **Max take-off weight** 2,041 kg (4,500 lb); **Payload** 758 kg (1,671 lb); **Empty weight** 1,283 kg (2,829 lb); **External load** N A; **Length** 9.93 m (32.6 ft); **Width** 1.98 m (6.5 ft); **Rotor diameter** 10.67 m (35 ft); **Height** 3.9 m (12.8 ft); **Max speed** 128 kt (237 km/h); **Cruise speed** 119 kt (220 km/h); **Service ceiling** N A; **Rate of climb** 7.6 m/sec (1,500 ft/min); **HIGE** 3,660 m (12,000 ft); **HOGE** N A; **Range** 330 nm (611 km); **Weapons** 4 × Stinger self-defence missiles

406 Combat Scout
The export version of the AeroScout

The prototype of what has become the 206/OH-58 series was first flown in 1962 as a competitor in the US Army's Light Observation Helicopter (LOH) programme, but lost to the Hughes OH-6A Cayuse (see separate entry); the helicopter in its TH-57A form was ordered by the US Navy and later was ordered for the US Army as the South-East Asian conflict started. Some 2,200 OH-58A Kiowas were delivered, whilst the OH-58C version has been assigned to the Light Infantry Divisions for flank security and scout roles, being armed from 1987-88 with the General Dynamics Stinger anti-aircraft missile; the C model has an uprated engine as well.

In September 1981, Bell won the (US) Army Helicopter

Aiming for the export market, the Bell 406 Combat Scout is armed here with 70 mm rockets and a 7.62 mm gun pod for combat support.

Improvement Programme (AHIP) competition and delivered the first re-modelled OH-58D, with mast-mounted sight, to the US Army in 1986; the helicopter is designed to operate in a 'fire team' with the McDonnell Douglas AH-64A Apache (see separate entry) but has yet to prove itself in anything but the artillery fire control role. Called the Aeroscout, the OH-58D has a very advanced cockpit and is available in the Model 406 Combat Scout export version, which is capable of taking the Hughes Aircraft TOW or the Saab-Emerson HeliTOW anti-tank missile system. Various nations also operate the basic commercial utility version for liaison, command and control, communications and other non-combat tasks, including training.

BELL 212/412 SERIES

First flight 16 April 1969 (212); 1979 (412); **Operational** 1970 (212); 1981 (412)

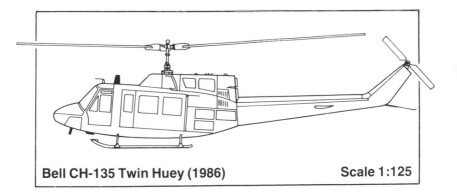

Bell CH-135 Twin Huey (1986) | Scale 1:125

UH-1N Twin Huey

Engines 2 × Pratt & Whitney of Canada PT6T-3B Twin Pac 1,800 shp (max cont power 1,600 shp); **Crew** 2; **Passengers** 13; **Max take-off weight** 5,080 kg (11,200 lb); **Payload** 2,360 kg (5,203 lb); **Empty weight** 2,720 kg (5,997 lb); **External load** 2,268 kg (5,000 lb); **Length** 13.99 m (45.9 ft); **Width** 2.86 m (9.4 ft); **Rotor diameter** 14.63 m (48 ft); **Height** 4.35 m (14.3 ft); **Max speed** 140 kt (259 km/h); **Cruise speed** 100 kt (185 km/h); **Service ceiling** 4,023 m (13,200 ft); **Rate of climb** 7.2 m/sec (1,420 ft/min); **HIGE** 3,350 m (11,000 ft); **HOGE** 2,835 m (9,300 ft); **Range** 224 nm (415 km); **Weapons** usually unarmed but can carry 2 × 7.62 mm machine guns or 70 mm rocket pods

CH-135 Twin Huey

The Canadian version

Soon to be flown by women, the Canadian forces' CH-135 is a VIP and SAR helicopter, a twin-engined Huey design (Bell).

Agusta-Bell 212
See separate entry

Harbin 212
The Chinese-assembled version

412
Engines 2 × Pratt & Whitney of Canada PT6T-3B-1 Twin Pac 1,400 shp;
Crew and Passengers as UH-1N; **Max take-off weight** 5,398 kg
(11,900 lb); **Payload** 2,500 kg (5,511 lb); **Empty weight** 2,964 kg (6,535
lb); **External load** 2,268 kg (5,000 lb); **Length, Width and Height** as
UH-1N; **Rotor diameter** 14.02 m (46 ft); **Max speed** 125 kt (232 km/h);
Cruise speed 122 kt (226 km/h); **Service ceiling** 4,970 m (16,300 ft);
Rate of climb 7.4 m/sec (1,450 ft/min); **HIGE** N A; **HOGE** 3,932 m
(12,900 ft); **Range** 228 nm (422 km); **Weapons** usually unarmed but
cleared for 70 mm rocket and machine gun pods

NBell 412
The IPTN Indonesian-built version

412SP
The special performance version

412 Griffon
The Italian version (see separate entry)

As a safety measure, it was decided to develop the UH-1 into a
twin-engined helicopter, especially for use by the Canadian Armed
Forces and the US Marine Corps, both operators having
considerable amounts of overwater flying to contend with during
normal operations. The Pratt & Whitney of Canada Twin Pac
powerplant was selected, particularly because of the Canadian
order, and the back-up systems are all dual-circuited for added
safety.

The US Air Force actually became the first user in 1970 when it
acquired nearly eighty UH-1N models for Special Operations
duties, particularly in South-East Asia but more recently in many
parts of the world, including Central America. The helicopter has
also been used by the 67th Aerospace Rescue and Recovery
Squadron (USAF) and to transport the US Navy's Seal diving
teams. The Canadian version was delivered 1971-72.

The UH-1N/212 series has been very successful in the world

market, being flown by 25 nations besides the United States and having been used operationally by Argentina, Israel, Peru (counter-insurgency), Sri Lanka and Uganda. In the late 1970s, Bell Helicopter Textron decided to improve the performance of the airframe with an uprated engine and, in conjunction with Agusta of Italy, to develop a four-bladed main rotor system of advanced technological design to enable the existing flight envelope to be opened.

The helicopter is produced under licence by IPTN of Bandung, Indonesia and Bell versions also serve with the Nigerian State Police, the Guatemalan and Panamian Air Forces and the 412SP version was sold to Norway in 1986.

BELL 214B/214ST SERIES

First flight 13 March 1974 (214A); 1980 (214ST); **Operational** 1975 (214A); 1982 (214ST)

214A Huey Plus
The developed Model 212 (see separate entry)

214A Isfahan
The Iranian co-funded version

214B Big Lifter
The aerial crane version

214C Isfahan
The special SAR version

Acquired by several South American nations, the Bell 214ST is derived from a US-Iranian programme doomed by the Shah's overthrow.

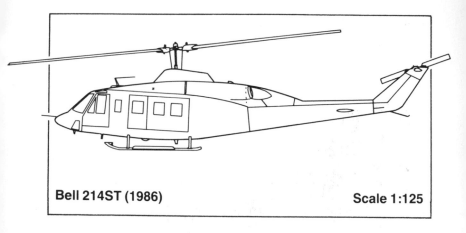

Bell 214ST (1986)   **Scale 1:125**

214ST SuperTransport

Engines 2 × General Electric CT7-2A 3,250 shp (max cont power 2,516 shp); **Crew** 2-3; **Passengers** 17-18; **Max take-off weight** 7,938 kg (17,500 lb); **Payload** 3,637 kg (8,019 lb); **Empty weight** 4,303 kg (9,487 lb); **External load** 3,583 kg (7,900 lb); **Length** 14.96 m (49.1 ft); **Width** 3.2 m (10.5 ft); **Rotor diameter** 15.9 m (52 ft); **Height** 4.3 m (14.2 ft); **Max speed** 140 kt (259 km/h); **Max cruise speed** 130 kt (241 km/h); **Service ceiling** 3,049 m (10,000 ft); **Rate of climb** 9 m/sec (1,780 ft/min); **HIGE** 1,950 m (6,400 ft); **HOGE** 304 m (1,000 ft); **Range** 450 nm (834 km); **Weapons** usually unarmed but cleared for 7.62 mm gun pods.

The original Huey Plus was a derivative of the Model 204/205/212 series but was designed to improve the helicopter's load carrying ability and its operation in hot/high locations, such as the Middle East. In fact, the major customer for the design remains the late Shah of Iran who ordered 293 of the 214A Isfahan tactical transports for the Imperial Iranian Army and 39 for the IIAF; since the overthrow of his regime several of the helicopters have been identified from television footage. The 214C SAR version remains in service in limited numbers.

The Bell 214ST (Stretched Twin or SuperTransport) was specifically developed for the Iranian market to form the basis of a helicopter industry with the possibility of exports around the Middle Eastern region. In the event, history overtook the design process and the 214ST was produced in Texas by Bell, selling to various US government customers including Dubai, Ecuador, Peru, the Philippines, Thailand and Venezuela.

BELL COBRA (SINGLE-ENGINE) SERIES

First flight 7 September 1965; **Operational** 1967

AH-1G Cobra
The initial production model of the Cobra; 1,078 built

AH-1Q Cobra
Converted to fire TOW missiles

AH-1S Modified Cobra
The AH-1Q with uprated engines

AH-1S Cobra
The production model, built to fire TOW

AH-1S Enhanced Cobra
The uprated production Cobra

AH-1S Modernised Cobra
Engine 1 × Lycoming T53-L-703 1,485 shp (max cont power 1,300 shp); **Crew** 1 pilot, 1 co-pilot/gunner; **Passengers** 0; **Max take-off weight** 4,535 kg (10,000 lb); **Payload** 1,543 kg (3,402 lb); **Empty weight** 2,993 kg (6,598 lb); **External load** N A; **Length** 13.59 m (44.6 ft); **Width** 3.27 m (10.75 ft); **Rotor diameter** 13.41 m (44 ft); **Height** 4.02 m (13.2 ft); **Max speed** 170 kt (315 km/h); **Max cruise speed** 128 kt (237 km/h); **Service ceiling** 3,718 m (12,200 ft); **Rate of climb** 8.3 m/sec (1,625 ft/min); **HIGE** 3,703 m (12,150 ft); **HOGE** 1,143 m (3,750 ft); **Range** 317 nm (587 km/h); **Weapons** (anti-tank) 1 × M197 20 mm cannon, 8 × TOW missiles; (close support/escort) 1 × M197 20 mm cannon, 4 × 70 mm rocket pods, or 4 × TOW and 2 × 70 mm rocket pods

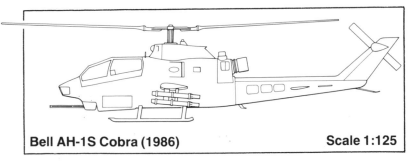

Bell AH-1S Cobra (1986)　　　　　**Scale 1:125**

The latest single-engined version of the Bell AH-1 Cobra is the TOW-armed and air data sensor-equipped S Model (Bell).

YAH-1S Cobra/TOW 2
A demonstration helicopter

PAH-2 Cobra
A contender for the Heeresflieger PAH-2 programme

In the early 1960s, Bell demonstrated its interest in the attack helicopter concept with the development of the Sioux Scout based on the Model 47 (see separate entry) and paved the way for the development of an armed helicopter to escort troop carrying machines into action. The Model 209 Cobra was actually eliminated from a US Army competition in 1965 but luckily for that nation, Bell continued its development as a private venture until resubmitted for US Army approval when the Vietnam War hotted up.

The design was based upon the Bell 204/UH-1 Huey series (see separate entry) and has been called the HueyCobra but is known by the US Army as the Cobra or Snake. It was originally armed with two 7.62 mm miniguns in the chin turret which was replaced by the M28 turret for M129 40 mm grenades or a combination of minigun and launcher. The stub wing pylons were fitted for four racks for 70 mm rocket pods, smoke grenade dispensers or minigun pods; a programme to introduce the 20 mm to the AH-1G was also undertaken. Several AH-1Gs were delivered to the USMC, Israel and Spain.

One hundred AH-1Gs were converted to Q standard to take the Hughes Aircraft TOW wire-guided anti-tank missile with a range of 3.75 km (2.3 miles) and several hundred further re-engined as AH-1S Modified Cobras, which can be identified by the angular canopy now common to all AH-1S models. Production AH-1S Cobras followed and 98 were built with enhanced armament and glass fibre rotor blades. By 1984, over 500 AH-1S Cobras had been upgraded to full AH-1S Modernised Cobra standard with laser range finder radar warning receivers, IR jammers and air data systems. This model will remain in service, updated with the Hughes Aircraft C-NITE night attack system for service from 1995 to 2005.

The AH-1G/S Cobra series has been exported with some success including Greece, Iran (used in action 1982/3), Israel (used in action in 1982), Japan (built under licence), Jordan (last delivered in 1985), Pakistan and Turkey. Production of this remarkable helicopter continues.

BELL TWIN-ENGINE COBRA SERIES

First flight 10 October 1969; **Operational** 12 February 1971

AH-1J SeaCobra

Engine 1 × United Aircraft of Canada T400-CP-400 Twin Pack 1,800 shp; **Crew** 1 pilot, 1 co-pilot/gunner; **Passengers** 0; **Max take-off weight** 4,536 kg (10,000 lb); **Payload** 1,127 kg (2,485 lb); **Empty weight** 2,998 kg (6,610 lb); **External load** N A; **Length** 13.94 m (45.75 ft); **Width** 2.2 m (7.17 ft); **Rotor diameter** 13.4 m (44 ft); **Height** 5.3 m (17.42 ft); **Max speed** 150 kt (278 km/h); **Max cruise speed** 140 kt (259 km/h); **Service ceiling** 4,877 m (16,000 ft); **Rate of climb** 8 m/sec (1,575 ft/min); **HIGE** 2,134 m (7,000 ft); **HOGE** 1,219 m (4,000 ft); **Range** 358 nm (663 km); **Weapons** (basic) 1 × 20 mm chin-mounted cannon, 2 × 70 mm rocket pods; (heavy attack) 1 × 20 mm chin-mounted cannon, 4 × 70 mm rocket pods

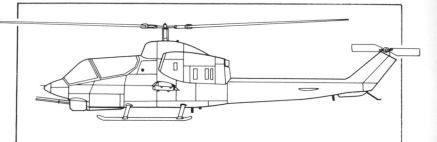

Bell AH-1J SeaCobra (1985)   **Scale 1:125**

AH-1J International SeaCobra
Sold to Iran

AH-1J SeaCobra TOW
The interim anti-armour version

AH-1T Improved SeaCobra
Engine 1 × Pratt & Whitney of Canada T400-WV-402 Twin Pac 2,050 shp; **Crew** as AH-1J; **Passengers** 0; **Max take-off weight** 6,350 kg (14,000 lb); **Payload** 1,509 kg (3,327 lb); **Empty weight** 3,880 kg (8,553 lb); **External load** N A; **Length** 13.9 m (45.58 ft); **Width** as AH-1J; **Rotor diameter** 14.6 m (48 ft); **Height** 4.17 m (13.67 ft); **Max speed** 180 kt (333 km/hr); **Max cruise speed** 142 kt (263 km/h); **Service ceiling** 3,794 m (12,450 ft); **Rate of climb** N A; **HIGE** 1,372 m (4,500 ft); **HOGE** 152 m (500 ft); **Range** 311 nm (576 km); **Weapons** (basic) 1 × 20 mm chin-mounted cannon, 2 × M229 70 mm rocket pods; (medium attack) 1 × 20 mm chin-mounted cannon, 8 × TOW; (heavy attack) 1 × 20 mm chin-mounted cannon, 8 × TOW, 2 × M229 70 mm rocket pods

AH-1T+ SuperCobra
The original name for the AH-1W

AH-1W SuperCobra
Engine 1 × General Electric T700-GE-401 Twin Pac 3,340 shp (max cont power 1,725 shp); **Crew** as AH-1J; **Passengers** 0; **Max take-off weight** 6,691 kg (14,750 lb); **Payload** 1,118 kg (2,465 lb); **Empty weight** 4,611 kg (10,165 lb); **External load** N A; **Length, Width, Rotor Diameter and Height** as AH-1T; **Max Speed** 170 kt (315 km/h); **Max cruise speed and Service ceiling** as AH-1T; **Rate of climb, HIGE and HOGE** N A; **Range** 300 nm (556 km); **Weapons** (basic) 1 × 20 mm chin-mounted cannon;

Just entering service with the US Marine Corps is the Hellfire-armed AH-1W SuperCobra which will be operated from ship or shore (Bell).

(LZ suppression) 1 × 20 mm chin-mounted cannon, 76 × 70 mm rockets, 16 × ZUNI 127 mm rockets or 2 × GPU-2A 20 mm gun pods; (basic anti-tank) 1 × 20 mm chin-mounted cannon, 8 × TOW, 2 × AIM-9G Sidewinder, or 2 × Stinger; (heavy anti-tank) 8 × Hellfire missiles carried instead of TOW

During the Vietnam War, the US Marine Corps requested a twin-engined attack helicopter which was capable of safe overwater operations, but based on the tried and tested AH-1G Cobra design. The result was the SeaCobra and 69 were built for the USMC but 202 were delivered to the Imperial Iranian Army prior to the Shah's overthrow. Most AH-1Js have been retired to the USMC Reserve.

The AH-1T was the improved dynamics helicopters, using the Bell 214 rotor system technology and capable of carrying the TOW anti-tank missile system. The first AH-1T Improved SeaCobra flew in May 1976 and over fifty were ordered for sea service. Another improvement plan was followed as the USMC entered the anti-helicopter combat era and wanted to use the Rockwell Hellfire laser-guided/designated anti-armour missile as the primary heavy combat weapon. The result was the re-engined AH-1T+ SuperCobra.

In 1985, Bell and USMC re-designated the helicopter as the AH-1W SuperCobra and 44 were ordered for service, with a further fifty AH-1T helicopters being brought up to W model standard after the new production helicopters have been delivered. The first AH-1W was delivered in March 1986.

BELL-BOEING TILT-ROTOR TEAM

V-22A OSPREY SERIES

XV-15
The tilt-rotor trials vehicle; two built

CV-22A Osprey
The special operations version

HV-22A Osprey
The US Navy SAR version

An artist's impression of the medical evacuation variant of the Bell-Boeing V-22A Osprey due to enter service in the early 1990s.

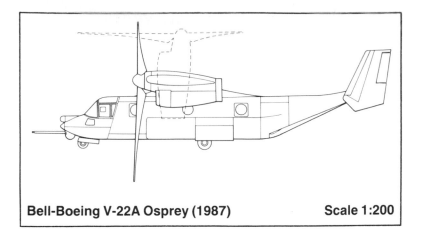

Bell-Boeing V-22A Osprey (1987)   **Scale 1:200**

MV-22A Osprey

Engines 2 × Allison M80C; **Crew** 2 pilots; **Passengers** 24; **Max take-off weight** 24,948 kg (55,000 lb); **Payload** 4,536 kg (10,000 lb); **Empty weight** N A; **External load** 4,536 kg (10,000 lb); **Length** 17.65 m (57.92 ft); **Width** 14.2 m (46.5 ft); **Rotor diameter** 11.6 m (38 ft); **Height** 6.63 m (12.75 ft); **Max speed** 350 kt (648 km/h); **Max cruise speed** 250 kt (463 km/h); **Service ceiling** 8,535 m (28,000 ft); **Rate of climb, HIGE and HOGE** N A; **Range** 400 nm (741 km); **Weapons** unarmed

SV-22A Osprey

The proposed US Navy ASW version

The US armed forces have a requirement for the following V-22 airframes: USN (combat rescue) 50; USMC (combat assault) 552; USAF (special operations) 80; US Army (long-range combat support) 231. The tilt-rotor concept of semi-helicopter and semi-fixed wing aircraft means that ideally the Osprey will replace the HH-3, CH-46, CH-53D, MC-130 and CH-47 during the period until 2005. The first V-22 is expected in service in 1992, with a first flight date of 1988. Until 1985, the design was known as the JVX — Joint Service Experimental Air Vehicle; the project has US Navy/US Marine Corps leadership.

The basic design of the tilt-rotor is a composite airframe, with advanced composite rotors with de-icing. The air vehicle (it is not really a helicopter but a convertiplane) has a high wing, with the tilting engines on either end connected by a drive shaft which can take power from either or both engines. The exhaust will include an infra-red suppressor and the engines have the ability to run dry should there be a leak of lubricant, either through mechanical failure or (more likely) because of enemy action.

The pilots may well have ejection seats and will have one of the most advanced cockpits yet designed. Included in the mission equipment is a pilot's night vision system, multi-mode radar and cathode ray tube (CRT) displays for systems, navigation and defences. The self-defence systems will include radar warning receivers and chaff dispensers. The V-22A can be refuelled in flight.

The V-22 is faster, travels further, higher and is better equipped when it reaches its target than any other helicopter. The USMC role requires that it carries 24 troops some 200 nm (370 km) radius of action, is shipboard compatible and can self-deploy worldwide. For the US Navy combat rescue role, the V-22 needs to be able to rescue four people up to 460 nm (852 km) radius of action at 250 kt (463 km/h) cruise speed. The special operations envisaged by the US Air Force will involve twelve troops being carried about 700 nm (1,296 km) radius of action and be capable of flying anywhere on earth. For full tactical flexibility, the US Army requirement is for a utility, medical evacuation and Corps area operations vehicle.

BOEING VERTOL HELICOPTER COMPANY

BOEING H-46 SERIES

First flight 22 April 1958 (H-46); May 1962 (KV-107); **Operational** 1962 (H-46); 1965 (KV-107)

YHC-1A
The prototype for US Army trials; became HRB-1 for USMC

YHC-1B
The developed version which became the H-47 (see separate entry)

CH-46A Sea Knight
The first production type

HH-46A Sea Knight
A rescue version

RH-46A Sea Knight
A one-off mine sweeping prototype

UH-46A Sea Knight
The USN vertical replenishment version

CH-46D Sea Knight
Engines 2 × General Electric T58-GE-16 1,870 shp; **Crew** 2 pilots, 1 aircrewman; **Passengers** 25; **Max take-off weight** 11,022 kg (24,300 lb); **Payload** 4,163 kg (9,179 lb); **Empty weight** 6,859 kg (15,121 lb); **External load** 4,356 kg (10,000 lb); **Length** 13.66 m (44.81 ft); **Width** 3.92 m (12.86 ft); **Rotor diameter** 15.24 m (50 ft); **Height** 5.09 m (16.69 ft); **Max speed** 145 kt (267 km/h); **Max cruise speed** 136 kt (252 km/h); **Service ceiling** 2,591 m (8,500 ft); **Rate of climb** 7.3 m/sec (1,433 ft/min); **HIGE** 3,200 m (10,500 ft); **HOGE** sea level; **Range** 180 nm (333 km); **Weapons** unarmed

UH-64D Sea Knight
The USN equivalent to the CH-46D

CH-46E Sea Knight
Has uprated engines and plastic rotor blades

UH-46E Sea Knight
Equivalent to CH-46E

CH-46F Sea Knight
Has undergone product improvement

CH-113 Labrador
Built as an SAR helicopter for the Canadian Armed Forces

CH-113A Voyageur
Built as troop transport for Canada

HKP-4A/B/C Sea Knight
Built for Sweden, powered by the Gnome engine

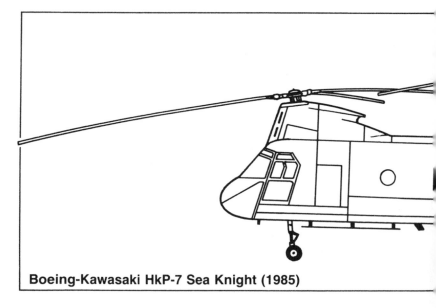

Boeing-Kawasaki HkP-7 Sea Knight (1985)

Built in Japan, the KV 107-II is a variant of the Boeing CH-46 family of maritime helicopters (Kawasaki).

Kawasaki KV-107 II

Built in several versions for the Japanese, Burmese, Thai and Saudi armed forces

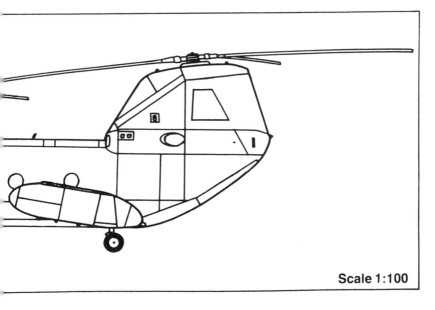

Scale 1:100

KV-107 IIA

Engines 2 × General Electric CT58-140-1 1,400 shp; **Crew and Passengers** as CH-46D; **Max take-off weight** 8,618 kg (19,000 lb); **Payload** 3,800 kg (8,377 lb); **Empty weight** 4,819 kg (10,623 lb); **External load** 5,216 kg (11,500 lb); **Length, Width, Rotor diameter and Height** as CH-46D; **Max speed** 146 kt (270 km/h); **Max cruise speed** 130 kt (241 km/h); **Service ceiling** 5,180 m (17,000 ft); **Rate of climb** 10.2 m/sec (2,000 ft/min); **HIGE** 3,353 m (11,000 ft); **HOGE** 2,438 m (8,000 ft); **Range** 190 nm (352 km); **Weapons** (anti-submarine) 6 × Type 51 depth charges, or 4 × Type 42 lightweight torpedoes (also carries Ericsson PS-8071 radar and lightweight dipping sonar)

The H-46 series began as a troop transport development for the US Army but when that service chose the larger H-47 Chinook, interest changed to the US Marine Corps and US Navy; both used the helicopter to good effect during the Vietnam War and it remains in service today, albeit in an improved version. Several experiments were carried out, including mine sweeping which was later taken up by the Japanese Maritime Self-Defence Force using the Kawasaki KV-107 II-3 variant from 1970.

For a Swedish requirement, the KV-107 was re-engined with the Rolls-Royce Gnome H1400 engine (in 1986, the T variant was retrofitted) and the helicopter has been operational against alien submarine activity in the Baltic. Japanese-built versions have also served with the Saudi para-military and armed forces.

The Canadian Voyageur fleet is used for SAR operations, being updated in 1982 to include nose-mounted search radar and other flying aids.

BOEING H-47 SERIES

First flight 21 September 1961; **Operational** April 1962

YHC-1B
The prototype derived from the H-46 (see separate entry)

CH-46A Chinook
The first US Army version

ACH-47A Go-Go-Bird
A fire suppression helicopter experiment

CH-47B Chinook
The uprated version

CH-47C Chinook
Engines 2 × Lycoming T55-L-712 3,750 shp (max cont power 3,000 shp); **Crew** 2 pilots, 1-2 aircrewmen; **Passengers** 44 (100+ carried standing); **Max take-off weight** 22,680 kg (50,000 lb); **Payload** 12,180 kg (26,851 lb); **Empty weight** 10,500 kg (23,149 lb); **External load** 12,700 kg (28,000 lb); **Length** 15.54 m (51 ft); **Width** 3.78 m (12.4 ft); **Rotor diameter** 18.3 m (60 ft); **Height** 5.68 m (18.7 ft); **Max speed** 160 kt (297 km/h); **Max cruise speed** 140 kt (259 km/h); **Service ceiling** 2,606 m (8,550 ft); **Rate of climb** 7.5 m/sec (1,485 ft/min); **HIGE** 2,499 m (8,200 ft); **HOGE** 1,798 m (5,900 ft); **Range** 229 nm (424 km); **Weapons** (self-defence) 7.62 mm GPMG, chaff dispensers

CH-47D Chinook
The re-worked helicopter for the US Army

CH-47J Chinook
The Japanese-built variant

Chinook HC 1
The British version, an interim C/D

CH-147 Chinook
The Canadian version

414 Chinook
The export version of the CH-46C

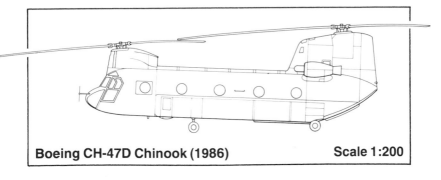

Boeing CH-47D Chinook (1986)   **Scale 1:200**

Operated by the Spanish FAMET (Army Light Aviation), the Boeing 414 International Chinook is a medium lift helicopter (Boeing).

International D Chinook
The new export version of the CH-47D

EMB-47C Chinook
The Italian built version of the CH-46D

In the late 1950s, the US Army required a troop transport helicopter in what was then classified as the heavy class (today it is medium lift), capable of carrying a platoon of 33 soldiers and their equipment across the battlefield. The Vertol design, drawing on previous company and Piasecki expertise, developed the tandem rotor Chinook which has become the standard medium lift helicopter of the Western world and continues in production.

Above *Carrying out a useful role as a search and rescue helicopter, this Aerospatiale Alouette III is operated by the Royal Danish Navy; note the use of floats rather than skid carriage (Paul Beaver).*

Below *Pictured over the French Mediterranean test area, the Aerospatiale AS 350B Ecureuil (left) in Gendarmerie colours with the AS 350L1 development helicopter armed with the Giat M621 20 mm cannon and 70 mm rockets in the foreground (Paul Beaver).*

Above *The Aerospatiale SA 366G1 Dolphin short range, rescue and recovery helicopter entered service with the US Coast Guard in 1985 and two of the first of the type delivered are pictured at CGAS New Orleans* (Paul Beaver).

Below *Assembled under licence in Singapore for the Singapore Air Force, this Aerospatiale AS 332L Super Puma departs on a training flight from Changi* (Paul Beaver).

Above *Showing off the latest colours for forward reconaissance helicopters with the UK Army Air Corps, this Westland-assembled Gazelle AH 1 is pictured at the AAC Centre, Middle Wallop, Hampshire (Paul Beaver).*

Below *Forming a smart line for a Sunday morning's parade, these Bell AH-1J SeaCobra helicopters are flown by the US Marine Corps Reserve (Paul Beaver).*

Above *A Boeing 414 Chinook medium lift helicopter at a Spanish FAMET airfield near Madrid refuelling and changing crew during an exercise (Paul Beaver).*

Below *Lurking in the trees on the Inner German Border, this MBB BO 105P is one of more than 200 which equip the Federal German Army's Heeresflieger. This helicopter is from 36th regiment at Fritzlar (Paul Beaver).*

During the Vietnam War the helicopter was used extensively as a load carrier to the fire support bases around the country, as well as carrying combat troops, and casualties and for recovering downed aircraft, sometimes under enemy fire. Several units were transferred to the Vietnamese armed forces but after the fall of Saigon in 1975 it is not thought that any remain in service.

In March 1967, the UK Royal Air Force requested the helicopter and a team was sent to St Louis to undertake the primary work but the project was cancelled only to be resurrected in 1978 when some 'spare cash' was found. Deliveries began to RAF Odiham in 1980 and in 1982 a number were sent to the Falkland Islands; only one survived the sinking of *Atlantic Conveyor* but this helicopter was used continuously during the campaign. During one operation it is credited with lifting 81 Gurhkas and since then over one hundred standing troops have been carried.

A production line was set up in Italy with deliveries of the EMB-47C being made to the Italian ALE, Morocco, Greece, Libya and Iran; the EMB-47Cs of the ALE will be updated to D standard in 1986-87, including the provision of plastic blades. Other Chinook users include Australia, Spain, Japan (where a third production line has been started), Argentina (which lost several in 1982), South Korea, Taiwan and Thailand. Nigeria ordered five but cancelled the project due to a lack of funding and the airframes were diverted to other contracts. Until the arrival of the EH 101, there is no rival on Western production lines.

EUROPEAN HELICOPTER INDUSTRIES

EH 101 SERIES

First flight March 1987; **Operational** November 1991

EH 101 Utility
The battlefield helicopter

EH 101 Naval

Engines 3 × General Electric T700-GE-401 2,275 shp (MMI); 3 × Rolls-Royce/Turbomeca RTM 322-01 2,500 shp (RN); **Crew** 1 pilot, 1 tactical commander, 2 observers (MMI); 1 pilot, 1 observer, 1 sonics operator (RN); **Passengers** 10; **Max take-off weight** 14,290 kg (31,500 lb; **Payload** 5,082 kg (11,204 lb); **Empty weight** 6,825 kg (15,046 lb); **External load** N A; **Length** 22.9 m (75.3 ft); **Width** N A; **Rotor diameter** 18.6 m (61 ft); **Height** 6.5 m (21.3 ft); **Max speed** 172 kt (319 km/h); **Max cruise speed** 164 kt (304 km/h); **Service ceiling** 2,000 m (6,562 ft); **Rate of climb** N A; **HIGE** N A; **HOGE** 1,463 m (4,800 ft); **Range** 1,100 nm (2,035 km); **Weapons** (anti-submarine) 4 × Mk46 (MMI) or Stingray (RN) lightweight torpedoes; 4 × Mk 11 depth bombs; (anti-ship) 4 × ASM

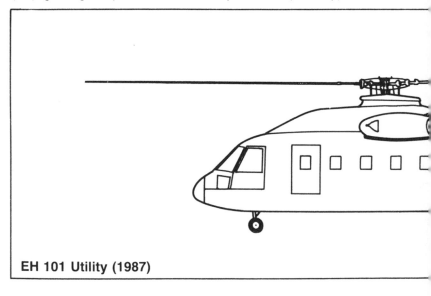

EH 101 Utility (1987)

Shown in Italian MMI (navy) markings in this artist's impression, the EH 101 is the Sea King/Lynx replacement for the Royal Navy also.

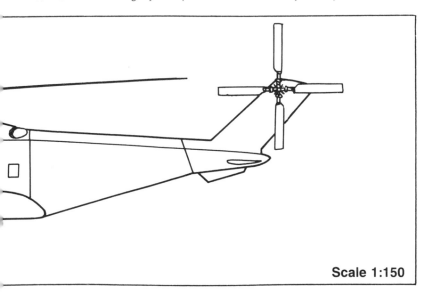

Scale 1:150

The EH 101 is a unique international co-operation venture between Italy (Agusta) and the United Kingdom (Westland) to provide a new generation helicopter for the Italian Navy (MMI) and the Royal Navy (RN). Originally proposed to both as a Sea King replacement, in the Royal Navy the helicopter will be given a small ships' role initially in conjunction with the towed-array frigates of the Type 23 and similar designs.

The first flight is scheduled to take place at Yeovil in early 1987 with the helicopter having been co-produced between the two companies under the leadership of the joint project office of EH Industries in London. Flight simulation is being used to decide upon the final cockpit and systems integration but it seems likely that the MMI will operate the helicopter afloat and ashore using a single pilot and a tactical commander (with some pilot skills) in the cockpit and two systems operators in the back. The Italian EH 101 will be equipped with the Bendix/British Aerospace FIAR Helras dipping sonar but as yet the RN version is scheduled to have deployable sonobuoys only. Both versions will be armed with lightweight torpedoes and other anti-submarine weapons but it seems likely that anti-shipping missiles will also be carried in due course. The naval version has considerable export potential as a Sea King replacement.

For the battlefield, it is highly possible that the British Army could acquire the helicopter as its next medium lift helicopter, powered by the RTM 322 engines suggested for the Royal Navy. In the utility role, the helicopter is fitted with a rear access ramp to take two light vehicles or 28 troops with two aircrewmen; the battlefield version would be crewed by two pilots. In this role, the EH 101 will be in direct competition with the Boeing 360 (a composite Chinook development) and the Bell-Boeing V-22A Osprey (see separate entry).

It is proposed to fit the EH 101 with a number of specialist systems from new, including a mission management computer, health monitoring and test equipment for the onboard systems such as the rotor dynamics, main gearbox and engines. The cockpit will feature a high degree of automation with an advanced coupled digital autopilot and full de-icing capability.

KAMAN AEROSPACE CORPORATION

KAMAN SH-2 SERIES

First flight 2 July 1959; **Operational** 1962

HU2K-1 Seasprite
The original design

UH-2A Seasprite
The first production variant

UH-2B Seasprite
A less capable variant

Taking on fuel by transfer from the deck of a warship, this is the SH-2D Seasprite, equipped with MAD and long range fuel tanks (US Navy).

UH-2C Seasprite
The first twin-engined development

HH-2C
The combat rescue variant

HH-2D
The less armoured SAR version

SH-2D Seasprite
An interim ASW helicopter

YSH-2E Seasprite
The prototype for the LAMPS 1 programme

SH-2F Seasprite
Engines 2 × General Electric T58-GE-8F 1,350 shp (max cont power 1,025 shp); **Crew** 2 pilots, 2 operators; **Passengers** 1; **Max take-off weight** 6,124 kg (13,500 lb); **Payload** 2,930 kg (6,460 lb); **Empty weight** 3,193 kg (7,040 lb); **External load** 1,814 kg (4,000 lb); **Length** (folded) 11.68 m (38.32 ft); **Width** (folded) 3.73 m (12.25 ft); **Rotor diameter** 13.41 m (44 ft); **Height** 4.14 m (13.58 ft); **Max speed** 143 kt (265 km/h); **Max cruise speed** 130 kt (241 km/h); **Service ceiling** 6,860 m (22,500 ft); **Rate of climb** 12 m/sec (2,440 ft/min); **HIGE** 5,670 m (18,600 ft); **HOGE** 4,695 m (15,400 ft); **Range** 367 nm (679 km); **Weapons** 2 × Mk 46/50 lightweight torpedo

SH-2G
An improved version with two T700-GE-401 engines

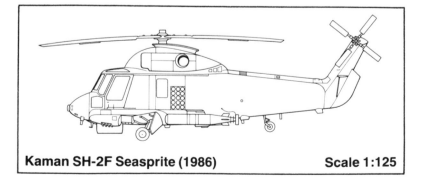

Kaman SH-2F Seasprite (1986)　　　　　**Scale 1:125**

The Kaman Seasprite started life as a single-engine long-range utility helicopter and by the mid-1980s has become a twin-engined lightweight anti-submarine warfare helicopter, part of the LAMPS-1 (Light Airborne Multi-Purpose System) for small warships where it acts as a systems and weapons platform but without any ability to act independently. The vulnerability of the single-engined UH-2 (powered by a GE T58 turboshaft) was converted into a twin-engined configuration between 1967 and 1970 during which period the helicopters were being used in the initial and often courageous combat rescue operations to rescue USN fixed-wing aircrew shot down over water and close to enemy-held territory. These helicopters were stationed close inshore on picket destroyers and capable of reacting extremely rapidly.

The first anti-submarine version of the Seasprite was the SH-2D which was declared operational in December 1971 and twenty airframes were converted from earlier variants whilst over a hundred of the later SH-2F were converted later. In addition, due to the late arrival of the SH-60B Seahawk (see separate entry) and because of the need to put ASW helicopters on most of the USN's new '600-ship fleet' developed under President Reagan, a new production line was opened at Kaman's New England plant. The production line should continue until 1989.

The SH-2F is fitted with a search radar in a chin mounting, carries deployable sonobuoys and ASW lightweight torpedoes, being vectored into position to engage submarines held in sonar contact by the parent ship or another sonar source. The helicopter can be used for over-the-horizon-targetting of ship-launched or air-launched missiles, as well as providing a platform for electronic warfare systems in defence of the naval task group. Plans have been announced in 1985 to offer a General Electric T700-GE-401 powered version to South Korea and Taiwan for shipborne helicopter requirements.

KAMOV DESIGN BUREAU

KAMOV KA-25 SERIES

First flight circa 1962; **Operational** circa 1965

Ka-20 Harp
The prototype ASW helicopter design

Ka-25 Hormone-A

Engines 2 × Glushenkov GTD-3F 900 shp; **Crew** 2 pilots, 1 flight engineer; 2 sonar operators; **Passengers** 12; **Max take-off weight** 7,500 kg (16,500 lb); **Payload** 2,735 kg (6,000 lb); **Empty weight** 4,765 kg

Operating a dipping sonar, this Ka-25 Hormone-A is also equipped with long range tanks and a sonobuoy dispenser (US DoD).

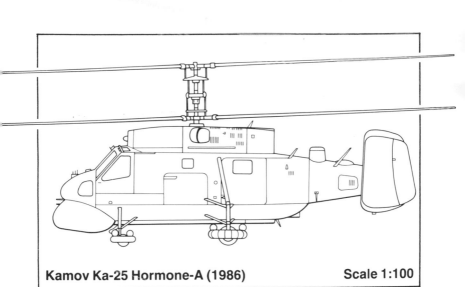

Kamov Ka-25 Hormone-A (1986)   **Scale 1:100**

(10,500 lb); **External load** N A; **Length** 9.75 m (32 ft); **Width** 3.76 m (12.35 ft); **Rotor diameter** 15.74 m (51.64 ft); **Height** 5.37 m (17.61 ft); **Max speed** 113 kt (209 km/h); **Max cruise speed** 104 kt (193 km/h); **Service ceiling** 3,500 m (11,500 ft); **Rate of climb, HIGE and HOGE** N A; **Range** 217 nm (400 km); **Weapons** (anti-submarine) 2 or 4 × lightweight torpedo, 6 × ASW mines/depth bombs

Ka-25 Hormone-B
The electronic warfare variant

Ka-25 Hormone-C
The vertical replenishment/SAR development

Ka-25K Hormone Crane
Briefly developed and then abandoned

The Kamov Design Bureau started naval helicopter designs for the Soviet forces with the Ka-15 (given the code-name Hen by NATO) which served from 1955-65, paving the way for the larger and more capable types which started with the Ka-20 Harp and led to the Ka-25 Hormone series, later developed further into the Ka-27 Helix (see separate entry). The Ka-20 was first seen in 1961 during a Soviet air show, being officially described as a rocket-carrying helicopter.

In 1967, the Soviets put the Ka-25 shipborne helicopter into international waters where it revealed some of its characteristics, including the co-axial rotor system and the twin turbine engines. The helicopter was developed into the Hormone-A which is a basic anti-submarine machine, with a nose-mounted search radar, anti-submarine weapons stored in a weapons bay and a deployable sonobuoy rack on either side of the fuselage.

The A was followed in the late 1960s by the B which was specially modified for electronic warfare, including the over-the-horizon-targetting of submarine-launched cruise missiles; it has the added feature of semi-retractable undercarriage, presumably to prevent interference with radar and EW systems. It does not appear to be armed.

The other main variant is the Hormone-C which is used aboard the 'Moskva' Class large anti-submarine cruisers and the later 'Kiev' Class airfraft carriers for 'plane guard, general SAR, communications and fleet liaison duties; it is thought to be capable of carrying ASW weapons. A typical helicopter air group aboard would be twelve to fourteen Hormone-As, three B models and two C models, although sixteen As and three Bs have been noted in the Mediterranean.

One source has indicated that as many as thirty sub-variants have been noted in operational service and presumably these include the Indian Naval version and those supplied to Syria, Vietnam and Yugoslavia. Production ceased in 1975 with the last deliveries thought to have been made to India.

KA-27/32 SERIES

First flight 1980 (Ka-27); Ka-32 (1981); **Operational** October 1981 (Ka-27); 1982-83 (Ka-32)

Ka-27 Helix-A

Engines 2 × Glushenkov TV-3 1,250 shp; **Crew** 2 pilots and 2 systems operators; **Passengers** 20; **Max take-off weight** 9,735 kg (21,462 lb); **Payload** N A; **Empty weight** 5,443 kg (12,000 lb); **External load** 4,990 kg (11,000 lb); **Length** 10.36 m (34 ft); **Width** 4.27 m (14 ft); **Rotor diameter** 15.74 m (51.64 ft); **Height** 5.49 m (18 ft); **Max speed** 120 kt (222 km/h); **Max cruise speed** 110 kt (204 km/h); **Service ceiling** 3,658 m (12,000 ft); **Rate of climb, HIGE and HOGE** N A; **Range** 270 nm (500 km); **Weapons** (anti-submarine) 2-4 × lightweight torpedo; or mines; or depth bombs; (anti-shipping) unguided rockets or guided missiles

Ka-27 Helix-B
Thought to be the vertical replenishment and SAR version

Ka-32 Helix
The civilian version

In February 1981, the Soviets announced through one of the official newspapers, *Red Star*, that a new SAR and reconnaissance helicopter had entered production under the designation Ka-32. The following October, NATO observers first identified a new helicopter aboard the warship, *Udaloy*, on deployment to the Baltic Sea and this was originally named the Ka-32 Helix by NATO but later the designation appears to have been notified by the Kamov OKB as Ka-27 for the military and Ka-32 for the civilian type.

In 1982 the first photographs were released to the western press and they showed a helicopter with a larger fuselage than the Ka-25 Hormone (see separate entry) which it is thought the Helix will replace by 1990. Certainly it is expected that Ka-27 is more capable than the older Ka-25, including having more advanced flight controls (a picture released at the Paris Air Show in 1985 showed the aircrew sitting in the rear cabin during flight!), the use of dipping sonar, more advanced sonobuoy deployment and possibly a simple onboard processor.

It appears that the Helix-A combines both roles of the A and B model Hormone, with the one helicopter having ASW and EW/OTHT operations roles, whilst the Helix-B (a presumed designation) including the ability to undertake SAR, vertrep and the transportation of naval infantry, even for limited assault operations. Some sources retain Helix-A for ASW and Helix-B for EW/OTHT with Helix-C for the SAR/vertrep version.

Future developments of the helicopter can include mines countermeasures (although the Mil-14 Haze-B seems to fulfil that role now — see separate entry— and anti-shipping strikes with unguided rockets and guided missiles. The latter would be particularly effective in countering surface action groups (SAGs) of missile-armed fast patrol boats and corvettes as found in the Mediterranean or off the African coast.

The helicopter has yet to be identified in operational service with any other Warsaw Pact or client state navy but it is possible that Syria could acquire the helicopter before 1990 as part of a reported naval build-up.

Kamov Ka-27 Helix-A (1986)   **Scale 1:100**

Operating from small and large warships, the Ka-27 Helix-A is the anti-submarine variant; note the chin-mounted radar.

MCDONNELL DOUGLAS HELICOPTER COMPANY

MCDONNELL DOUGLAS 500 SERIES

First flight 27 February 1963 (OH-6A); 4 May 1984 (530MG);
Operational 1966

369HM
The company designation for the 500 series

OH-6A Cayuse
The production scout for the US Army

*The light shipborne version of the McDonnell Douglas 500MD series
carring a MAD 'bird' and a single Mk 44 torpedo.*

Above *For several years, McDonnell Douglas Helicopter Company has been flying the NOTAR (NO TAil Rotor) system on a Model 500 demonstrator. This system may well be used for LHX* (McDonnell Douglas Helicopter Company).

Below *Seen on the California range is a McDonnell Douglas 500 Defender armed with a 7-round 70 mm rocket pod (port) and 12.7 mm FN Herstal machine gun pod* (Lear Siegler).

MH-6A Cayuse
The special operations version

OH-6C Cayuse
A special test vehicle

OH-6D Cayuse
A proposed advanced scout

OH-6J
The Japanese version from Kawasaki

500D
The training and liaison version of a civil design

500E
The improved communications design

500M
The export version of the OH-6A

500MD Defender
An export anti-tank helicopter

500MD ASW
An Italian-built version

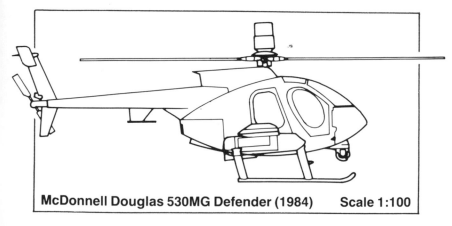

McDonnell Douglas 530MG Defender (1984)   **Scale 1:100**

530F Lifter

A high altitude version of the 500E

530MG Defender

Engine 1 × Allison 250-C30B 650 shp; **Crew** 1 pilot, 1 co-pilot/gunner; **Passengers** 1; **Max take-off weight** 1,361 kg (3,000 lb); **Payload** 559 kg (1,233 lb); **Empty weight** 801 kg (1,767 lb); **External load** 939 kg (2,070 lb); **Length** 9.3 m (30.5 ft); **Width** 2.1 m (6.8 ft); **Rotor diameter** 8.05 m (26.41 ft); **Height** 2.7 m (8.9 ft); **Max speed** 122 kt (226 km/h); **Max cruise speed** 119 kt (220 km/h); **Service ceiling** 4,877 m (16,000 ft); **Rate of climb** 10.5 m/sec (2,070 ft/min); **HIGE** 5,060 m (6,600 ft); **HOGE** 4,298 m (14,100 ft); **Range** 203 nm (376 km); **Weapons** (scout) 1 × 7.62 mm gun pod, 1 × 70 mm rocket pod; (close support) 2 × TOW missiles, 1 × 7.62 mm gun pod; (anti-tank) 4 × TOW

NH-500 Series

Produced under licence in Italy by Breda-Nardi

RACA-500 Series

Produced under licence in Argentina

The agile, fast and effective Hughes 500 series has seen operational service in Vietnam, Laos, Grenada, Honduras, El Salvador and Iraq (where some twenty 530MF variants were delivered in 1986); it is also reported that eighty 500D models were illegally exported to North Korea in 1983-84 despite a US government embargo. This latter action is ironic because Korean Airlines is responsible for the manufacture of large parts of the 500 airframe and may take over the complete production run in 1988.

Since the first OH-6A Light Observation Helicopter entered service, the airframe has been developed into an anti-tank helicopter which saw service in the Israeli invasion of Lebanon and during the Kenyan officers rebellion in 1982. In 1984, the 530MG version was shown for the first time at the Farnborough Air Show where its Hughes Aircraft mast-mounted sight, forward looking infra-red (FLIR) and Racal Avionics mission management system with cathode ray tube displays were admired. As yet there have been no orders for this version but the more cost-effective 500/530 Nightfox helicopter, with commercial FLIR and the provision of light machine guns might well become a successful seller in the Latin American and South-East Asian markets. Other weapons include the provision of Stinger for self-defence and the Hughes chain gun. The Hughes Helicopter company was purchased by McDonnell Douglas in 1984 and changed its name to McDonnell Douglas in 1985.

MCDONNELL DOUGLAS AH-64 SERIES

First flight 30 September 1975; **Operational** April 1986

YAH-64 Apache
The prototype advanced attack helicopter

AH-64A Apache
Engines 2 × General Electric T700-GE-701 1,690 shp (max cont power 1,536 shp); **Crew** 1 pilot, 1 co-pilot/gunner; **Passengers** 0; **Max take-off weight** 9,318 kg (20,500 lb); **Payload** 4,327 kg (9,520 lb); **Empty weight** 4,991 kg (10,980 lb); **External load** N A; **Length** 14.97 m (49.11 ft); **Width** 5.23 m (17.16 ft); **Rotor diameter** 14.63 m (48 ft); **Height** 4.22 m (13.84 ft); **Max speed** 197 kt (378 km/h); **Max cruise speed** 145 kt (268 km/h); **Service ceiling** 6,250 m (20,500 ft); **Rate of climb** 14.6 m/sec (2,880 ft/min); **HIGE** 4,633 m (15,200 ft); **HOGE** 3,780 m (12,400 ft); **Range** 330 nm (611 km); **Weapons** (standard) 1 × XM230E 30 mm chain gun; (anti-tank defence) 8 × Hellfire laser-guided missiles; (air cavalry) 8 × Hellfire, 36 × 70 mm rockets; (escort) 76 × 70 mm rockets

Pictured during firing trials of the Rockwell Hellfire laser-designed anti-tank missile, this is the AH-64A Apache (Hughes Helicopters Inc).

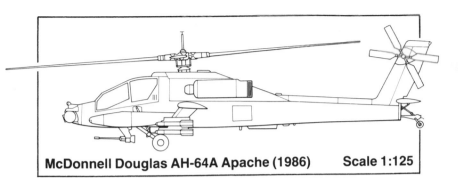

McDonnell Douglas AH-64A Apache (1986)   **Scale 1:125**

AH-64B Apache
The proposed advanced cockpit and system helicopter

Designed to meet the needs of the US Army in Europe and the Middle East for an advanced attack helicopter capable of all-weather day/night anti-tank operations in a hostile area, against enemy fire and the winner of the 1973-76 advanced attack helicopter programme, the Apache began entering service with US Cavalry units at Fort Hood, Texas in April 1986. It is planned to bring the first units to Europe in 1988 by which time design work will have been completed on the updated AH-64B version which besides advanced avionics might be powered by Rolls-Royce/ Turbomeca RTM 322 engines and be armed with the Stinger air-to-air missile for self-defence.

The Apache brought to the US Army the ability to operate across the enemy's front line to destroy tank and armoured vehicle concentrations which necessitated a large number of survivability features being built into the design, including a gearbox which can run for 30 minutes without lubrication and two self-contained aircrew 'capsules'. The gunner in the front of the tandem seats is equipped with the TADS (Target Acquisition and Designation System) whilst the pilot uses the PNVS (Pilot's Night Vision System) for battlefield operations.

The helicopter is armed with the 30 mm chain gun as standard, capable of carrying between 1,200 and 250 rounds depending on the density altitude and the tasking. In addition the standard 70 mm Hydra unguided rockets can be carried but the main weapon is the Rockwell Hellfire laser-guided anti-armour missile with a range in excess of Soviet air defences. In battle, the Apache would operate with the Bell OH-58D Aeroscout (see separate entry) in fire teams in blunt and divert enemy armoured thrusts. Covering fire can be provided by the 30 mm chain gun and it is possible that the Stinger missile system will be fitted although the scout helicopter may well be the only recipient in order that the Apache crews concentrate on 'killing' tanks.

The Apache has been designed for self-deployment but can also be accommodated in the USAF C-5A Galaxy (6) or the C-141A Starlifter (2) for long-range deployment. On several occasions the helicopter has been deployed to Europe via the northern (Iceland) or southern (Azores) routes. The first AH-64A National Guard unit forms in 1987 and there are possible Israeli and Federal German Heeresflieger requirements.

MESSERSCHMITT-BÖLKOW-BLOHM

MBB BO 105 SERIES

First flight 16 February 1967; **Operational** 1975

BO 105C
The liaison and communications version

BO 105C (Naval)
The shipboard version

BO 105CB
Civilian training and liaison version

BO 105CBS
The stretched version

BO 105M
The military observation and liaison

The observation version of the CASA-built BO 105P series in service with Sapin's FAMET; gunship and missile-armed versions were also built.

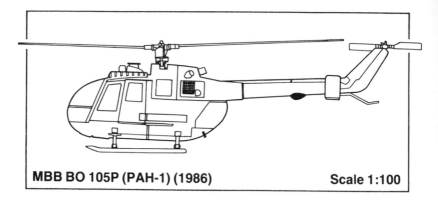

MBB BO 105P (PAH-1) (1986)   **Scale 1:100**

BO 105P

Engines 2 × Allison 250-C20B 420 shp (max cont power 400 shp); **Crew** 1 pilot, 1 observer; **Passengers** 1; **Max take-off weight** 2,400 kg (5,291 lb); **Payload** 942 kg (2,076 lb); **Empty weight** 1,458 kg (3,215 lb); **External load** 1,000 kg (2,204 lb); **Length** 8.56 m (20.08 ft); **Width** 2.5 m (8.25 ft); **Rotor diameter** 9.84 m (32.28 ft); **Height** 3 m (9.84 ft); **Max speed** 145 kt (270 km/h); **Max cruise speed** 113 kt (210 km/h); **Service ceiling** 3,000 m (9,845 ft); **Rate of climb** 7 m/sec (1,378 ft/min); **HIGE** N A; **HOGE** 1,000 m (3,280 ft); **Range** 407 nm (754 km); **Weapons** (anti-tank) 6 × HOT/HOT-2 anti-tank missiles (4-8 × HeliTOW for Sweden); (close support) 1 × Rh 202 20 mm cannon

Casa BO 105

The Spanish-built version

HkP 9A

The Swedish anti-tank version

HkP 9B

The Swedish SAR version

NBO-105

The Indonesian-built version

Initially developed for the civilian helicopter market, the BO 105 design has been successful in entering and capturing much of the light attack helicopter market in Europe with examples in service with the Spanish FAMET in anti-tank, close support and light observation roles, with the Federal German Heeresflieger for liaison, training and communication (VBH) as well as for anti-tank operations (PAH-1). The Swedes have recently taken delivery of the Saab HeliTOW equipped version of the BO 105C known as the HkP 9A.

In 1974, the Federal German Bundeswehr selected the BO 105M as the VBH helicopter and ordered one hundred (which were delivered by 1983) and in 1975, after deciding to procure an interim anti-tank helicopter, the BO 105P (or PAH-1 Panzer Abwehr Hubschrauber) was ordered with a total of 212 delivered by September 1984. The PAH-1 equips three regiments supporting the First (GE) Corps in the NATO Central Front and a divisional unit in northern Germany. The PAH-1 is armed with the Euromissile HOT (soon to be HOT-2) wire-guided anti-tank missile with a range of 3,750 m (2.3 miles), using the SFIM APX 397 direct view sight. The helicopter also has an uprated transmission and improved tail rotor to allow the schwarme (platoon-sized units) to hover in ambush for enemy tanks crossing the North German Plain. In 1987, the first PAH-1 units will start to receive night vison goggles but it will be some time before a full night firing capability can be assured along the lines of the Swedish Hkp 9A's Saab HeliTOW system, the first in the world.

Export operators include Indonesia (one hundred built locally), Iraq and Spain (CASA-built), Mexico and Columbia (naval), Peru, the Netherlands (30 BO 105 observation helos), Nigeria (24 BO 105 SAR, operated by the air force) and the Philippines.

MBB/KAWASAKI BK 117 SERIES

BK 117A-3
The liaison and VIP version

BK 117A-3M

Engines 2 × Avco Lycoming LTS 101-650 B-1 550 shp (410 kW); **Crew** 1-2 pilots; **Passengers** 10; **Max take-off weight** 3,200 kg (7,055 lb); **Payload** 1,505 kg (3,318 lb); **Empty weight** 1,695 kg (3,737 lb); **External load** as Payload; **Length** 9.88 m (32.41 ft); **Width** 2.75 m (9.02 ft); **Rotor diameter** 11 m (36.08 ft); **Height** 3.3 m (10.82 ft); **Max speed** 150 kt (278 km/h); **Max cruise speed** 136 kt (252 km/h); **Service ceiling** 4,500 m (14,760 ft); **Rate of climb** 9.9 m/sec (1,950 ft/min); **HIGE** 3,000

Carrying eight HOT missiles and mounting both a mast-mounted sight and the Lucas 12.7 mm gun turret, this is the BK 117A-3M demonstrator.

m (9,850 ft); **HOGE** 2,500 m (8,200 ft); **Range** 270 nm (500 km); **Weapons** (anti-tank) 8 × TOW or HOT wire-guided missiles; (close support) 2/4 × 70 mm rocket pods, 1 × 12.7 mm chin-mounted Lucas gun turret; (scout) 2 × 7.62 mm/12.7 mm gun pods

Although the Japo-German designed BK 117 had been ordered for para-military operations by the Ciskei government and the Spanish Gardia Civil, it was not until the Paris Air Show 1985 that the first truly military version of the helicopter, the A-3M, was unveiled. This helicopter is a multi-role or combat support helicopter with the ability to carry out a quick role in the event that a military situation changes and thus the concept appeals to those nations requiring several types of helicopter but only being able to afford one. Flight tests began in mid-1986.

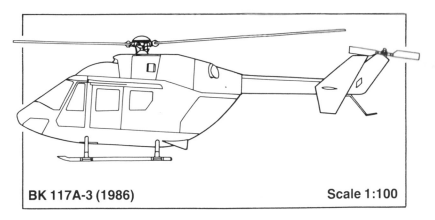

BK 117A-3 (1986)   **Scale 1:100**

The agility and speed of the BK 117A-3 has also impressed the US Army and one has been delivered for trials in air-to-air helicopter combat currently being undertaken in several places in the US.

To provide self-defence, the BK 117A-3M is fitted with advanced radar and laser warning receivers and the Lucas 12.7 mm gun turret which is mounted under the nose, linked to the pilot's helmet-mounted sight, thus being able to train onto an air or ground target during a battle engagement. It is possible that the helicopter could be configured to take the General Dynamics air-launched Stinger missile or the planned Shorts Starstreak self-defence hyper-velocity hitile.

For anti-tank operations, the A-3M can be fitted with either the TOW or HOT wire-guided systems, using a conventional direct view optical sight in the cabin roof or a television-linked mast-mounted sight high above the main rotor system. In addition to missiles, the standard 70 mm fin-folding aerial rockets from the US or Europe can be used by the helicopter for ground fire suppression and limited anti-vehicle operations.

In the trooping role, the large rear cabin with its four doors (two clam-shells aft, under the tailboom and two either side of the fuselage) can be used for rapid deplaning from the helicopter, especially important in hostile landing zones, under fire. The helicopter has only a minimum of survivability equipment and systems fitted, emphasizing the limited war role and the cost-effectiveness in the design. A major battlefield conflict would undoubtedly call for dedicated anti-tank or close support helicopters.

MIL DESIGN BUREAU

Mi-1 SERIES

First flight 1948; **Operational** 1951

Mi-1 Hare

Engine 1 × Ivchenko A1-26V radial 575 hp; **Crew** 1-2 pilots; **Passengers** 2-3; **Max take-off weight** 2,460 kg (5,425 lb); **Payload** 500 kg (1,102 lb); **Empty weight** 1,760 kg (3,880 lb); **External load** N A; **Length** 12.1 m (39.69 ft); **Width** N A; **Rotor diameter** 14.35 m (47.08 ft); **Height** 3.3 m (10.83 ft); **Max speed** 92 kt (170 km/h); **Max cruise speed** 76 kt (140 km/h); **Service ceiling** 3,000 m (9,840 ft); **Rate of climb** 5.3 m/sec (1,043 ft/min); **HIGE and HOGE** N A; **Range** 321 nm (600 km); **Weapons** (training) unarmed; (reconnaissance) 1 × 7.62 mm/12.7 mm machine gun

Mi-1NKh Hare
The government version

Mi-1S Hare
The Soviet-built ambulance version

Mi-1T Hare
The utility version

Mi-1U Hare
The purpose-built training version

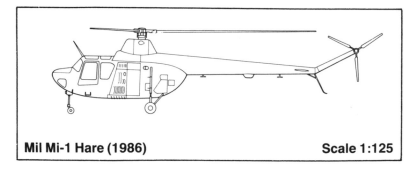

Mil Mi-1 Hare (1986)   **Scale 1:125**

Operated by many para-military organizations besides the Soviet armed forces, the Mi-1 Hare was the USSR's first successful helicopter (Novosti Press Agency).

Mi-1UT Hare
The specialist flying school version

SM-1 Hare
The Polish-built Mi-1

SM-1W Hare
The improved version

SM-1WS Hare
The casualty evacuation version

SM-1SZ Hare
The purpose-built training version

SM-2 Hare
A development version

The Mi-1 is the first design to be successfully produced by the design bureau (OKB) of the late Mikhail Mil and was conceived in 1947 as a light utility and training helicopter for the Soviet forces. The helicopter has been very successful and has even won the World Helicopter Championships for the USSR.

The Mi-1's earliest version were fitted with a wood-metal main rotor blade but this was amended in later versions, including the WSK (Wytwornia Sprzetu Komunikacyjnego) SM-1W which was part of a very large Polish production run. In fact, in order that Soviet factories could concentrate on later models, the Mi-1 production appears to have been moved to Poland in 1961 which allowed the Swidnik factory to develop the helicopter design into the SM-1 series. This was followed by the SM-2, a five-seater with a 15 per cent increase in payload and larger diameter main rotor blades.

Some experiments were carried out in the late 1950s to use the helicopter for anti-tank operations with early wire-guided missile variants. It is thought that although this gave the Soviet forces valuable experience with the helicopter systems, the Mi-1 was not deemed operational with missiles. However bearing in mind the maxim that all Soviet helicopters are armed on the battlefield, it is thought that the Mi-1 is operational in the USSR and elsewhere with the 7.62 mm or 12.7 mm machine gun, strapped to the fuselage side. An example was photographed in Poland with a weapon attachment point although it was bearing 'civilian' markings.

Operators of the Mi-1 outside the USSR include Bulgaria, China (People's Republic), Cuba, Czechoslovakia, Egypt, East Germany, Hungary, Iraq, Mongolia, Poland and Yugoslavia.

MI-2 SERIES

First flight 1961; **Operational** 1964

Pictured in the Libyan desert, this Mil Mi-2 Hoplite is carrying long-range ferry tanks but no weapons.

Mi-2 Hoplite

Engines 2 × Istotov GTD-350P 450 shp; **Crew** 1-2 pilots; **Passengers** 7-8; **Max take-off weight** 3,700 kg (8,157 lb); **Payload** 1,328 kg (2,928 lb); **Empty weight** 2,372 kg (5,229 lb); **External load** 800 kg (1,763 lb); **Length** 11.94 m (39.17 ft); **Width** 3.05 m (10 ft); **Rotor diameter** 14.56 m (47.76 ft); **Height** 3.75 m (12.3 ft); **Max speed** 113 kt (210 km/h); **Max cruise speed** 108 kt (200 km/h); **Service ceiling** 4,000 m (13,125 ft); **Rate of climb** 4.5 m/sec (885 ft/min); **HIGE** 2,000 m (6,560 ft); **HOGE** 1,000 m (3,280 ft); **Range** 237 nm (440 km); **Weapons** (training and utility) unarmed; (anti-tank) 4 × AT-3 guided missiles or unguided rockets; (close support) 1 × 23 mm cannon

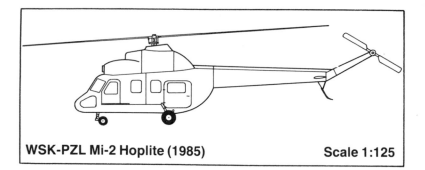

WSK-PZL Mi-2 Hoplite (1985)　　　　　**Scale 1:125**

Mi-2M Hoplite
A twelve seat utility version

Mi-2R Hoplite
The air ambulance version

WSK-PZL Kania
The Allison 250-C20B-powered development

WSK-PZL Sokol
The fourteen seat development

In the late 1950s, the Mil OKB commenced work on a re-engining of the Mi-1 which would reduce the helicopter's empty weight to payload ratio, especially in relation to the engine/transmission. It hoped to do this by using a turboshaft engine arrangement using much of the Mi-1's systems. The helicopter first flew in 1961 but before it gained operational status with the Soviet armed forces, a Soviet-Polish helicopter manufacturing agreement had been signed to allow WSK-PZL to undertake all production and future development work. Between November 1965 and September 1979, three thousand Mi-2s had been built for various customers in the Swidnik factory.

As far as is known some 25 variants of the Mi-2 have been built including armed versions for anti-tank operations using the AT-3 Sagger and other Soviet systems, or for close support carrying unguided rockets and gun packs. In the forward observation and scouting role, the helicopter is obviously outdated but it still provides useful service as utility transport and as a training helicopter in one of the many quasi-military 'sports' training academies around the Soviet Union and the Warsaw Pact. In the Mi-2R air ambulance configuration, four stretchers can be carried together with a flight nurse; this version has many para-military duties.

Internal developments in Poland have included the re-engining of the basic Mi-2 design with the Allison 250-C20B engine to provide the Kania which was seen at the Hannover Air Fair in 1984 and there is the possibility of an enlarged version to carry fourteen passengers and to be called the Sokol. Although intended for the civilian market, neither design is expected to sell in the West which already has enough low technology helicopters of this size; there are however possibilities for the military in the Warsaw Pact although recent Mil design (see separate entry for new designs) has probably robbed the WSK-PZL organization of any success with the developments.

The Mi-2 is operated by many nations outside the Warsaw Pact including Albania, Syria and Yemen.

Mi-4 SERIES

First flight August 1952; **Operational** 1953

Mi-4 Hound-A

Engine 1 × Shvetsov Ash-82V 1,700 hp (max cont power 1,350 hp); **Crew** 2 pilots; **Passengers** 14; **Max take-off weight** 7,800 kg (17,200 lb); **Payload** 1,740 kg (3,836 lb); **Empty weight** 5,392 kg (11,887 lb); **External load** 1,300 kg (2,866 lb); **Length** 16.8 m (55.11 ft); **Width** 3.82 m (12.5 ft); **Rotor diameter** 21 m (68.89 ft); **Height** 5.18 m (17 ft); **Max speed** 113 kt (210 km/h); **Max cruise speed** 90 kt (167 km/h); **Service ceiling** 5,500 m (18,000 ft); **Rate of climb, HIGE and HOGE** N A; **Range** 217 nm (400 km); **Weapons** (utility) 1 × 12.7 mm forward fire machine gun; (close support) 1 × 12.7 mm machine gun, 4 × rocket pods

Mi-4 Hound-B
The naval version with ASW weapons

Mi-4 Hound-C
The electronic warfare version

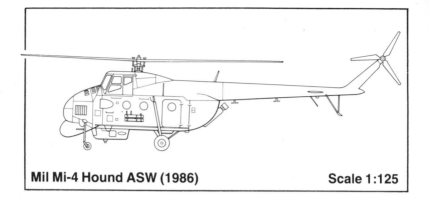

Mil Mi-4 Hound ASW (1986) **Scale 1:125**

Mi-4L Hound
The VIP transport

Mi-4P Hound
The commercial passenger version

Mi-4S Hound
The agricultural version

Harbin Z-5
The Chinese-built version

Harbin Z-6
The proposed turbine-powered version

The Mi-4 put the Soviet helicopter industry in the forefront of international helicopter design in the early 1950s and although the helicopter has been generally superceded by later types, such as the Mi-8 (see separate entry), the Hound (the NATO reporting name) continues in widespread service around the world. It was the first Soviet helicopter to fly with an hydraulic flight control system and the helicopter widely reported to have been designed, built and test flown within seven months.

The Mi-4 was the first Soviet helicopter capable of massed infantry attack and it could carry either fourteen fully-armed troops or a small cross-country vehicle. Later the helicopters were fitted with fire suppression armament including the 12.7 mm machine gun and unguided rockets mounted on fuselage outrigger racks.

Above *Visiting picturesque Castle Ashby in central England, this Polish-built Mil Mi-2 Hoplite training helicopter is operated by the para-military national air training organization and was taking part in the 1986 World Helicopter Championships* (Paul Beaver).

Below *Disappearing into the smoke of battle is the Sikorsky H-76 Eagle multi-role helicopter which was announced at the 1985 Paris Air Show* (Sikorsky).

Above *Moving in to collect US and Egyptian troops during Exercise Bright Star, the Sikorsky UH-60A Black Hawk is a versatile helicopter* (US DoD).

Below *Pictured during operations off Lebanon in 1983, this Sikorsky CH-53D Sea Stallion is one of the heavy lift helicopters of the US Marine Corps* (US DoD).

Above *Landing at the Toulon naval air station in the south of France, this Westland Lynx Mk 4 is normally embarked aboard 'corvettes' of the Mediterranean Fleet (Paul Beaver).*

Below *Operated afloat and ashore, the Westland Lynx Mk 89 is flown by the Nigerian Navy (Paul Beaver).*

Above *Rounding Table Mountain, Cape Town, is a Westland Wasp flown by the South African Air Force for search and rescue operations* (Herman Potgieter).

Below *Pictured in Norway during winter training for the UK's Royal Marines, these Westland Wessex HU 5s have now been phased out of front line service but still operate in SAR and communications duties* (Paul Beaver).

Operated by several air forces, the Mil Mi-4 was the first transport helicopter in service with the USSR; this is a Finnish example (F. J. Bachofner).

In about 1956, the Soviet Navy took a keen interest in the helicopter resulting in what NATO calls the Hound-B version for shore-based anti-submarine warfare, carrying nose-mounted search radar, a deployment magnetic anomaly detector (MAD), racks for sonobuoys and a weapons bay for mines, depth bombs and anti-submarine lightweight torpedoes. Very few remain in front-line Soviet AV-MF service but a few continue to operate in training roles and with client states.

To provide electronic warfare, both surveillance and counter–measures, the Soviet air force fitted the Hound with various equipment and NATO has given the helicopter the designation Hound-C. The helicopter probably does not directly compare with NATO equivalents but there are certainly more of them.

Production has also been carried out in the People's Republic of China and there have been a series of plans to re-engine the helicopter, known locally as the H-5, with a western high technology turboshaft twin-pack engine but this has been abandoned in favour of western airframes.

Mi-6 SERIES

First flight 1957; **Operational** 1960

Mi-6 Hook-A

Engines 2 × Soloviev D-25V (TV-2BM) 5,500 shp; **Crew** 2 pilots, 1 flight engineer, 1 navigator and 1 load master; **Passengers** 65; **Max take-off weight** 42,502 kg (93,700 lb); **Payload** 15,262 kg (33,645 lb); **Empty weight** 27,240 kg (60,055 lb); **External load** 8,000 kg (17,637 lb); **Length** 33.18 m (108,85 ft); **Width** 15.3 m (50.19 ft); **Rotor diameter** 35 m (114.82 ft); **Height** 9.86 m (32.34 ft); **Max speed** 162 kt (300 km/h); **Max cruise speed** 135 kt (250 km/h); **Service ceiling** 4,500 m (14,750 ft); **Rate of climb, HIGE and HOGE** N A; **Range** 334 nm (620 km); **Weapons** (utility) 12.7 mm forward firing machine gun; (air assault) 1 × 23 mm cannon

When it was announced in 1957, the Mi-6 (NATO name Hook) was the largest helicopter flying anywhere in the world and it has the distinction of being the first Soviet helicopter with turbine engines, the first twin turbine helicopter, the first helicopter to fly in excess

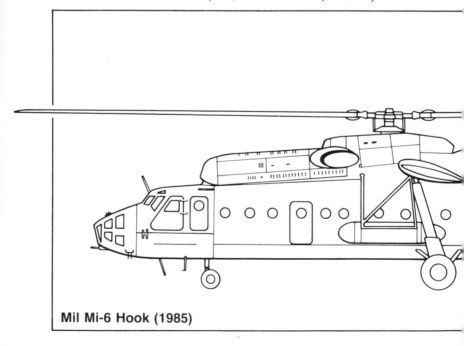

Mil Mi-6 Hook (1985)

Pictured in Egypt, this is the Mi-6 Hook, passing a Westland Commando during routine training (Peter Scott/Rolls Royce).

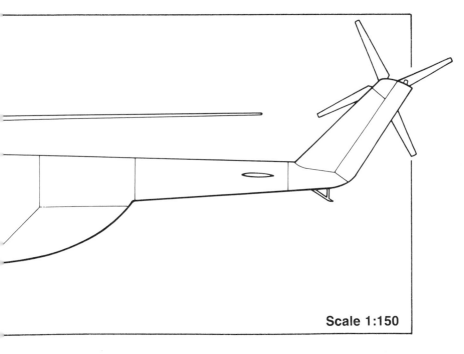

Scale 1:150

of 130 km/h (162 kt) and the largest gearbox then flying, weighing about 3,175 kg (7,000 lb) — that is heavier than the max all-up weight of the Mi-1.

A closely guarded secret during its development, the Mi-6 helped to shape Soviet military posture at home and around the world, being capable of landing heavily armed troops in large numbers, together with direct fire weapons, such as field artillery and missile launchers, over a large radius of action. The Mi-6 was delivered to various client states including Egypt where it was used to move anti-aircraft missile sites in the desert and to (North) Vietnam for the same role, with some being used across into South Vietnam to carry field artillery into the mountains overlooking US and South Vietnamese bases.

The Hip has recently been in action, during the Ethiopian operations against first Somalia and then against guerrilla forces in Eritrea and of course a large number have been deployed with the so-called 'limited contingent of Soviet forces' in Afghanistan. Most recently, camouflaged Mi-6s were seen at the Chernobyl nuclear disaster site moving concrete and other materials over the burning nuclear reactor using a long line method of carrying the loads.

Western sources credit the Soviet helicopter industry with completing about 800 Hooks and it is thought that 300 remain in Soviet air force service but that a number have been transferred to Aeroflot for government work in Siberia and to the KGB for moving listening posts and other intelligence equipment to remote sites facing the People's Republic of China and the NATO nations. Bulgaria seems to have been the only Warsaw Pact nation to have received the helicopter, although it does operate with Group of Soviet Forces, Germany.

The helicopter can be fitted with characteristic wings for forward flight enhancement but these are usually removed for aerial crane and heavy load lifting work. In Poland the helicopter is operated by Instal, the domestic airline and several have been noted recovering cosmonauts in Soviet Asia.

Mi-8/17 SERIES

First flight 1961 (Mi-8A), 1962 (Mi-8C), 1980 (Mi-17); **Operational** 1967 (Mi-8), 1981 (Mi-17)

Armed to the teeth, the Mil Mi-8 Hip-E is a formidable assault helicopter and capable of sustained anti-tank operations (US DoD).

Mi-8 Hip-A
The first prototype version with a single engine

Mi-8 Hip-B
The second prototype with two engines

Mi-8 Hip-C
The first production version

Mi-8 Hip-D
The command and control version

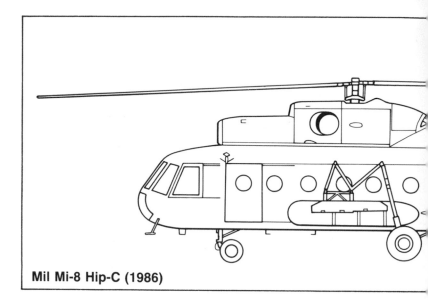

Mil Mi-8 Hip-C (1986)

Mi-8 Hip-E

Engines 2 × Isotov TV2-117A 1,700 shp; **Crew** 2 pilots, 1 flight engineer/loadmaster; **Passengers** 32; **Max take-off weight** 12,000 kg (26, 455 lb); **Payload** 5,376 kg (11,852 lb); **Empty weight** 6,624 kg (14,603 lb); **External load** 3,000 kg (6,614 lb); **Length** 18.17 m (59.61 ft); **Width** 4.5 m (14.76 ft); **Rotor diameter** 21.29 m (69.84 ft); **Height** 5.65 m (18.53 ft); **Max speed** 140 kt (260 km/h); **Max cruise speed** 122 kt (225 km/h); **Service ceiling** 4,500 m (14,760 ft); **Rate of climb** N A; **HIGE** 1,900 m (6,233 ft); **HOGE** 800 m (2,625 ft); **Range** 251 nm (465 km); **Weapons** (anti-tank/assault) 4 × AT-2 Swatter missiles, 6 × 57 mm rocket pods

Mi-8 Hip-F

The export version of the E, armed with six AT-3 Sagger

Mi-8 Hip-G/J/K

Electronic warfare versions

Mi-8P

The commercial version for 24 passengers with square windows

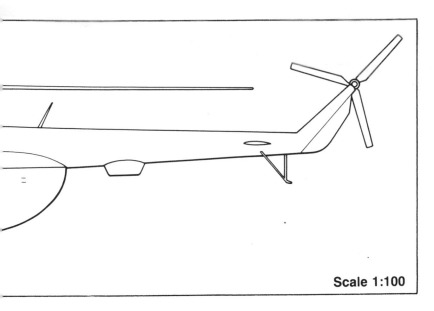

Scale 1:100

Mi-8T
The quick change civil/military version

Mi-17 Hip-H
The improved version

After more than twenty years in production, the Mi-8 series is still being produced by Soviet state aircraft factories at a rate of more than twenty a month, mainly for export but also to make up attrition losses from Afghanistan where the guerrillas have taken a heavy toll. The main production type now appears to be the Mi-17 (or Hip-H) with more powerful engines and better performance margins; it carries a 12.7 mm machine gun mounted aft through the rear clam-shell cargo doors.

The Mi-8 (called Hip by NATO) is in widespread service, having operated around the world from the mountains of Peru to the antarctic wastes, from Africa to China where it has been built under licence. The Mi-8 began the move towards air mobility for Soviet ground forces and contributed to the development of the armed military helicopter which has led to the development of the Mi-24 (see separate entry). In addition, through its naval operations, especially in mines clearance during the operations in the Suez

Canal zone during 1974, a naval variant began development which culminated with the Mi-14 (see separate entry).

For the NATO ground defences in Europe, one of the primary threats is the rocket and missile armed Hip, capable of carrying more than 24 troops and operating in a *desant* fashion to capture rear areas, such as airfields, command posts and rear supply echelons. This type of role was demonstrated in the 1973 Yom Kippur war when large numbers of Egyptian Hips, carrying commando teams, led the way across the Suez Canal and when Syrian Hips attacked the Golan Heights. In the Ogaden war, Soviet/Cuban-led forces from Ethiopia penetrated the Somali lines and captured gun positions from behind. The exact number of Hips in the Warsaw Pact forces is not known but they must exceed 5,000 as some 8,000 Mi-8 variants have been built.

Mi-14 SERIES

First flight 1974; Operational 1975

Mi-14 Haze-A

Engines 2 × Isotov TV3-116 2,200 shp; **Crew** 2 pilots, 2 systems operators; **Passengers** 24; **Max take-off weight** 10,886 kg (24,000 lb); **Payload, Empty weight and External load** N A; **Length** 18.29 m (60 ft); **Width** 4.5 m (14.75 ft); **Rotor diameter** 21.34 m (70 ft); **Height** N A; **Max speed** 150 kt (278 km/h); **Max cruise speed** 135 kt (250 km/h); **Service ceiling** 4,572 m (15,000 ft); **Rate of climb, HIGE and HOGE** N A; **Range** 240 nm (445 km); **Weapons** (anti-submarine) lightweight torpedoes, mines and depth charges

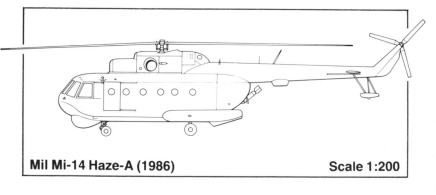

Mil Mi-14 Haze-A (1986)　　　　　　　　　　**Scale 1:200**

Operating in Polish colours this Mi-14 Haze is shown using its amphibious hull during an exercise with naval ASW units.

Mi-14 Haze-B
The mines countermeasures version

Mi-14 Haze-C
Could be the export version

Developed from the Mi-8 and the Mi-24 (see separate entries), the Mi-14 is a shore-based maritime helicopter which appears to have a primary role of defending the large Soviet Red Banner Fleet submarine installations in the White, Baltic and Black Seas and aiding the undetectable departure of Soviet ballistic missile carrying submarines from these ports. It has replaced the majority of Mi-4 Hound-B helicopters in service but does not appear to have been tested at sea except in the Haze-B version which seems to be a naval mines countermeasures helicopter rather in the guise of the RH-53D Sea Stallion/MH-53E Sea Dragon helicopters (see separate entry) of the US Navy.

Development probably began in 1968 using the basic Hip airframe which was modified into almost a brand new type, powered by Isotov TV3-117 engines which are used for the Mi-17/Mi-24 programmes. The use of the boat hull and retractable undercarriage are interesting and recently a number of photographs of the Haze on the sea's surface have been released; it is possible that dipping sonar could be used in this position.

The development of the Ka-27 Helix (see separate entry) would appear to confirm that the Mi-14 will remain as a shore-based helicopter, mainly dictated by its large dimensions which might not allow it to fit through the flight deck lifts of even the new nuclear-powered aircraft carriers. The helicopter's basic equipment consists of a Doppler navigation system, deployable MAD 'bird' sensor which is flown behind the helicopter in level flight and used to detect slight variations in the Earth's magnetic signature which could mean that a large submarine is below, deployable passive sonobuoys which listen for even the smallest sounds, a chin-mounted search radar (probably the same type as the Ka-27) and a fuselage weapons bay for the standard variety of ASW weapons.

Export of the Mi-14 has not been great, but it is thought that helicopters (possibly now designated Haze-C by NATO) have been delivered to Libya (although they have not been reported in action with US Naval forces in 1986), Poland and Bulgaria. East Germany and Syria might be the next customers, especially as the latter has announced the formation of a submarine force. The helicopter is destined to remain in service for many years.

Mi-24 SERIES

First flight 1971; **Operational** 1972

Mi-24 Hind-A

Engines 2 × Isotov TV2-117A 1,500 shp; **Crew** 1 pilot, 1 gunner; **Passengers** 8-10 troops; **Max take-off weight** 8,400 kg (18,520 lb); **Payload** 1,700 kg (3,748 lb); **Empty weight** 4,700 kg (10,360 lb); **External load** N A; **Length** 17 m (55.8 ft); **Width** 3.66 m (12 ft); **Rotor diameter** 21.34 m (70 ft); **Height** 4.25 m (14 ft); **Max speed** 157 kt (290 km/h); **Max cruise speed** 147 kt (273 km/h); **Service ceiling** 3,048 m (10,000 ft); **Rate of climb** 12 m/sec (2,362 ft/min); **HIGE and HOGE** N A; **Range** 240 nm (445 km); **Weapons** (standard) 1 × 12.7 mm

The first of the famous Mi-24 series was the Hind-A, armed here with 57 mm rocket launchers and the anti-tank missile rails clean.

trainable machine gun; (assault) 2 × AT-2 Swatter and 4 × 57 mm rocket pods, with 8-10 troops; (anti-tank) 4 × AT-2 Swatter and 4 × 57 mm rocket pods with extra fuel.

Mi-24 Hind-B
The initial production variant with four weapons points

Mi-24 Hind-C
An unarmed training version

Mi-24 Hind-D
Engines 2 × Isotov TV3-117 2,200 shp; **Crew** 1 pilot, 1 gunner, 1 flight engineer; **Passengers** 8-10 troops; **Max take-off weight** 10,000 kg (22,045 lb); **Payload** 2,000 kg (4,409 lb); **Empty weight** 6,500 kg (14,330 lb); **External load** N A; **Length** 18.5 m (60.7 ft); **Width and Height** as Hind-A; **Rotor diameter** 17 m (55.78 ft); **Max speed** 170 kt (315 km/h); **Max cruise speed** 150 kt (278 km/h); **Service ceiling** as

Operated by Warsaw Pact and Soviet client states the Mi-24 Hind-D has become the most famous Soviet helicopter design; this one is Czech (W. W. Duck).

Hind-A; **Rate of climb** 15.2 m/sec (3,000 ft/min); **HIGE and HOGE** N A; **Range** 250 nm (463 km); **Weapons** (standard) 1 × 3 12.7 mm nose-mounted Gatling machine gun; (assault/anti-tank) 4 × AT-2 Swatter guided missiles and 4 × 57 mm rocket pods with 8/10 troops (assault only)

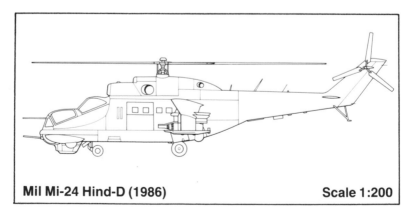

Mil Mi-24 Hind-D (1986)   **Scale 1:200**

Mi-24 Hind-E

Details as Hind-D except **Weapons** (standard) 1 × 23 mm GSU-23 cannon; (anti-tank) 4 × AT-6 Spiral guided missiles and 4 × 57 mm rocket pods; not intended to carry troops

Mi-24 Hind-F

(Presumed designation). Details as Hind-D except **Weapons** (standard) 1 × 2 23 mm fuselage-mounted cannon; (anti-tank) 4 × AT-6 Spiral and 4 × 57 mm rocket pods; (anti-helicopter) 4 × AT-6 Spiral with anti-air modifications plus 4 × 57 mm rocket pods; not intended to carry troops

Mi-25

The export designation for the Hind series

The remarkable flying artillery piece known to the Soviets as the Sturmovik (after the famous Second World War fighter-bomber) or Hunchback, to NATO as Hind, and to the Afghan rebels as Flying Death is a remarkable helicopter but its performance has tended to be over-emphasized. Battles with Chinese troops in 1969 seem to indicate the first plans to develop a flying assault weapon capable of securing an area with massive fire power and of landing assault troops to hold ground, using the vertical take-off characteristics of the helicopter.

The Mil OKB's Mi-24 design was prepared for testing in several prototype forms during 1971, with emphasis being placed on speed, aerodynamic shape, self-defence/survivability and the ability to carry a powerful weapons load, including radio-guided anti-tank missiles which could also be used against ground targets. In the later Hind-E and F versions, the AT-6 Spiral fin-folding guided missile appears to have the ability to engage helicopters and other low flying aircraft and this, together with a 23 mm cannon has led NATO planners to consider anti-helicopter helicopters and self-defence systems to defend against the marauding Hind concept.

Operationally, the Hind has been most active in Afghanistan, where several hundred have been employed with great success despite losing some 120 to rebel fire, thus emphasizing the large numbers employed and the fact that the helicopter was not designed to operate in the hot/high conditions of that mountainous nation. Special tactics have been evolved to use the helicopters to protect trooping helicopters and aircraft by dropping large numbers of IR decoy flares which are a countermeasure to IR-seeker missiles like the Redeye and SA-7 Grail used by the Afghans. In addition, Angola has been using the Mi-25 Hind against UNITA rebels but as yet there have been no reports of contact with South African forces although UNITA claims the destruction of about twenty of the helicopters to ground fire. In Central America, the Americans see the introduction of the Mi-25 to Nicaragua as an escalation of the guerilla war and in Iraq the helicopter has been used to good effect against dug-in Iranian positions. The Hinds are apparently used in tank-style emplacements because they do not have the ability to hover and engage targets with rockets or missiles; this is apparently because of the Russian terrain's lack of suitable cover for a hovering helicopter.

In Soviet service, the Hind arrived in East Germany and tactics were quickly developed, including the use of the cabin to carry extra rockets and missiles rather than troops. Basically the D, E and F models do not carry troops, but rather work in conjunction with the Hip-E.

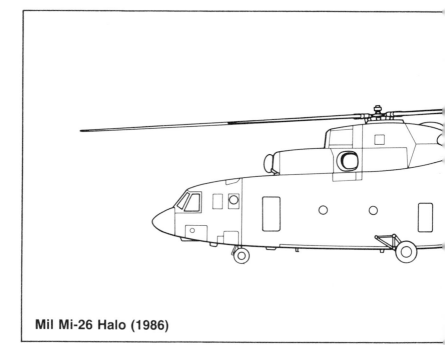

Mil Mi-26 Halo (1986)

Mi-26 SERIES

First flight 14 December 1977; **Operational** 1980

Mi-26 Halo-A

Engines 2 × Lotarev D-136 11,400 shp; **Crew** 2 pilots, 1 flight engineer, 1 navigator, 1 load master; **Passengers** 40-70 troops; **Max take-off weight** 56,000 kg (123,450 lb); **Payload** 27,800 kg (61,280 lb); **Empty weight** 28,200 kg (62,170 lb); **External load** 20,000 kg (44,090 lb); **Length** 33.72 m (110.62 ft); **Width** 8.95 m (29.36 ft); **Rotor diameter** 32 m (105 ft); **Height** 8.05 m (26.42 ft); **Max speed** 159 kt (295 km/h); **Max cruise speed** 137 kt (255 km/h); **Service ceiling** 4,500 m (14,760 ft); **Rate of climb and HIGE** N A; **HOGE** 1,800 m (5,900 ft); **Range** 432 nm (800 km); **Weapons** unarmed

This remarkable helicopter is the largest rotary-wing aircraft in production in the world and in sheer size is quite awe inspiring; the cargo hold is only a little smaller than that of a C-130 Hercules

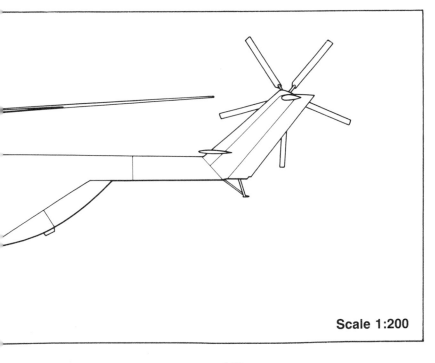

Scale 1:200

Seen at the Paris Air Show, the Mi-26 is the largest helicopter in the world and has been used operationally in Afghanistan.

transport aircraft and the tail rotor has a greater diameter than the main rotor of the McDonnell Douglas 530MG (see separate entry). The Mi-26 is looked upon as a replacement for the Mi-6 Hook (see separate entry) mainly for civilian purposes connected with the development of Siberia and central Asia, but with the Afghanistan war it was inevitable that the helicopter should be sent to Afghanistan; according to *Defence Helicopter World*, a unit of Mi-26 were deployed in 1983-84 when the Guerillas had cut much of the road traffic.

In military terms, the ability of the Mi-26 to carry 20,000 kg over 800 km at 255 km/h makes it a worthwhile battlefield transport with the ability to operate where conventional fixed-wing aircraft could not land. Recent press newsreel footage shows the Mi-26 operating with camouflage markings in Afghanistan and it was photographed again during the Chernobyl nuclear disaster.

In the cockpit, which is spacious, there is provision for the captain and co-pilot, with a flight engineer and navigation behind respectively. Much of the instrumentation is simple, conventional and lacking in clear order but the view from the windows would easily allow external load lifting from confined sites. Also in the cockpit is a jump-seat for an extra aircrewman and four additional seats on the cargo bay bulkhead. When flying the Mi-26 gives an overriding impression of quietness from the outside but with no sound insulation present in either demonstration aircraft at Paris (1981 and 1985) or Farnborough (1984), the Mi-26's internal noise would be uncomfortable.

According to recent analysis, the Mi-26 is a load lifter rather than a trooper (the seats appear uncomfortable and there are only a total of seven fuselage windows), being capable of lifting such weapon systems as the ZSU-23-4 self-propelled anti-aircraft artillery, armoured personnel carriers and the small PT-76 amphibious tank. Access to the cargo bay is via two clam-shell doors.

It is probable that the Mi-26 Halo will replace the Mi-6 in Soviet regimental service (only) during the next five to ten years.

Mi-28 SERIES

First flight 1981 (?); **Operational** 1986 (?)

Mi-28 Havoc

Engines 2 × Isotev TV3-117 2,500 shp (max cont power 2,200 shp); **Crew** 1 pilot, 1 co-pilot/gunner; **Passengers** 0; **Max take-off weight, Payload, Empty weight and External load** N A; **Length** 17.4 m (57.08 ft); **Width** 1.8 m (5.9 ft); **Rotor diameter** 17 m (55.75 ft); **Height** N A; **Max speed** 162 kt (300 km/h); **Max cruise speed** 145 kt (269 km/h); **Service ceiling** 3,658 m (12,000 ft); **Rate of climb** 18 m/sec (9,144 ft/min); **HIGE** 3,658 m (12,000 ft); **HOGE** N A; **Range** 259 km (480 km); **Weapons** 1 × 23 mm cannon undernose, 16 × new generation missiles, 2 × air-to-air missiles

The US Department of Defense believes that the Mi-28 Havoc will enter service in regimental numbers under 1987 but that it has been tested in Afghanistan during 1985-86 as part of the development programme, pre-service introduction to Group of Soviet Forces Germany. The whole concept of the Havoc (NATO code-name) seems to be based on the US Army's advanced

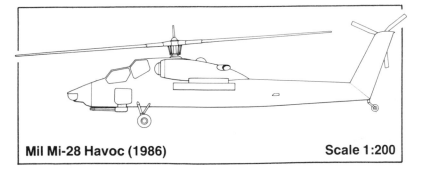

Mil Mi-28 Havoc (1986)　　　　　　　　　　**Scale 1:200**

An artist's impression of the Soviet advanced attack helicopter called Havoc by NATO; note the array of armament (US DoD).

attack helicopter with the basic roles of anti-tank operations, close support for ground forces, anti-helicopter operations against NATO anti-tank helicopters, armed reconnaissance and attacking command posts and the like. In these roles, the Mi-28 would be supported by armed Mi-8 and Mi-24 helicopters (see separate entries).

The basic armament seems to be, according to drawings produced by the US Army, the 23 mm cannon mounted under the nose in a gondola with perhaps 600 rounds of ammunition. For anti-tank operations, the Americans say the helicopter is armed with a laser-guided/designated version of the tube-launched AT-6 Spiral up to a maximum of sixteen rounds and still have capacity to carry two or four SA-14 Mod air-to-air infra-red homing missiles. For self-protection and battlefield survivability the Mi-28 is probably equipped with a pulse radar (thimble on the nose), forward looking infra-red (FLIR), direct view sight, radar warning receivers and perhaps even a mission management system with digital maps; it certainly has a Doppler navigation system, say Washington-based sources.

The new missiles have a range against tanks of about 6,000 m (3.72 miles) which equates to about 33 per cent better TOW-2, the best in NATO until the Hellfire system is fully operational in Europe. The anti-helicopter and anti-low flying aircraft modified SA-18 would indicate that the marauding Havoc will pose a greater threat to NATO helicopter forces than the existing marauding Hind. The Mi-28 has the ability to take the battle over the forward line of own troops in all weathers, day or night.

SCHWEIZER AIRCRAFT CORPORATION

SCHWEIZER/HUGHES TH-300C

First flight October 1956; **Operational** November 1964

TH-55A Osage
The primary trainer for the US Army

Hughes 300C
The commercial version sold for export

Schweizer TH-300C
The proposed Porsche-engined variant

Schweizer H-300C

Engine 1 × Lycoming H10-360-D1A 190 hp; **Crew** 1 instructor, 1 pupil; **Passengers** 1; **Max take-off weight** 930 kg (2,050 lb); **Payload** 431 kg (950 lb); **Empty weight** 499 kg (1,100 lb); **External load** 476 kg (1,050 lb); **Length** 9.4 m (30.83 ft); **Width** 1.99 m (6.52 ft); **Rotor diameter** 8.2 m (26.8 ft); **Height** 2.65 m (8.69 ft); **Max speed** 91 kt (145 km/h); **Max cruise speed** 83 kt (153 km/h); **Service ceiling** 3.109 m (10,200 ft); **Rate of climb** 3.8 m/sec (750 ft/min); **HIGE** 1,829 m (6,000 ft); **HOGE** 823 m (26.8 ft); **Range** 200 nm (370 km); **Weapons** unarmed

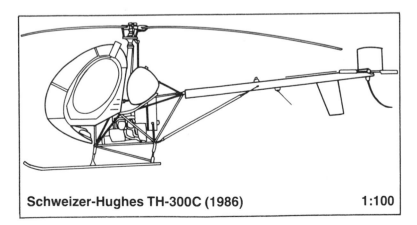

Schweizer-Hughes TH-300C (1986)   1:100

The US army continues to use the Schweizer-Hughes TH-55A Osage for basic helicopter pilot training (Northrop).

Beginning life as a commercial training and agricultural helicopter, the Hughes Helicopters Model 269 was of immediate interest to the US Army and in 1964 it selected the 269A to be the new primary trainer, a two-seat helicopter. The TH-55A Osage entered service in November 1964 and was used to train a large number of US Army and other service pilots going to Vietnam; in addition, under NATO and bi-lateral training agreements a large number of foreign pilots learned to fly on the helicopter.

The helicopter is small, light and very simple. The welded steel tail is fitted to the plexiglass bubble cabin, with the piston engine sitting behind. The helicopter has been widely exported and is used by a large number of airborne law enforcement agencies in the United States.

In 1985, the Federal German Heeresflieger issued a requirement for a new training helicopter to replace the existing Alouette II (see separate entry) and one of the responses was from the Schweizer company (which had taken over the Hughes 300C production/spares support in 1983). In 1986, at the Hannover Air Show, it was announced that the Heeresflieger bid would probably include the provision of the German-built Porsche radial piston engine as powerplant if the TH-300C design won the competition.

About 250 TH-55A Osage helicopters remain in service with the US Army, according to *Defence Helicopter World*, the leading military helicopter trade journal.

SIKORSKY AIRCRAFT

SIKORSKY S-58 SERIES

First flight 8 March 1954 (HSS-1), 8 March 1970 (S-58T); **Operational** August 1955 (HSS-1), 1971 (S-58T)

HSS-1 SeaBat
The initial version for the US Navy

HUS-1 SeaHorse
The utility version for the US Marines

H-34A Choctaw
The initial version for the US Army

CH-34C Choctaw
Saw service with the USAF, US Army and for export

VH-34C
The US Presidential helicopter

S-58T
Engines 2 × Pratt & Whitney PT6T Twin Pac 1,625 shp; **Crew** 2 pilots, 1 load master; **Passengers** 17-18; **Max take-off weight** 5,896 kg (13,000 lb); **Payload** 2,495 kg (5,500 lb); **Empty weight** 3,402 kg (7,500 lb); **External load** 2,268 kg (5,000 lb); **Length** 14.2 m (46.5 ft); **Width** 3.6 m (12 ft); **Rotor diameter** 17.1 m (56 ft); **Height** 4.4 m (14.3 ft); **Max speed** 117 kt (212 km/h); **Max cruise speed** 110 kt (204 km/h); **Service ceiling** 3,658 m (12,000 ft); **Rate of climb** 6.5 m/sec (1,275 ft/min); **HIGE** 3,170 m (10,400 ft); **HOGE** 1,980 m (6,500 ft); **Range** 260 nm (482 km); **Weapons** generally unarmed but can carry 7.62 mm gun pods

In the early 1950s, the US Navy issued a requirement for a new naval anti-submarine helicopter and the HSS-1/H-34 was the result of the design work carried out by United Technologies Sikorsky Aircraft Division, using the Wright R-1820 radial piston engine as the powerplant. The helicopter was rapidly adopted by several forces including the French who were engaged in operations against the guerilla forces of Algerian independence at the time; the operations carried out by the French led to the development of the armed helicopter. The helicopter was built under licence in France by Sud-Est, one of the forerunners of Aerospatiale.

The S-58 series was operated by almost all facets of the US armed forces and carried out operations in many locations, including Antarctica and the jungles of South-East Asia. On re-equipping its own forces with other types, the US military disposed of the surplus helicopters to some 25 nations for transport duties. Today, almost twenty years later, a handful remain in service with several nations, including Thailand and Uruguay.

In the late 1960s, it was decided to re-engine the S-58 along the lines of the turbine-powered Westland Wessex (see separate entry) and the result was the S-58T. In the early 1980s, Sikorsky Aircraft sold the rights and the spare parts to California Helicopters which company still markets and supports the design today. S-58T users include the Thai, Philippines and Indonesian armed forces with several new conversions being acquired annually. The helicopter is destined to continue in service while stocks of spares last because it is cost-effective to operate and the Twin Pac engines are so reliable.

Demonstrating the trooping and close support roles of the Sikorsky-California Helicopters S-58T.

Sikorsky (California Helicopters) S-58T (1986)

Scale 1:125

SIKORSKY S-61 SERIES

First flight 11 March 1959; **Operational** September 1961

HH-3A Sea King
A search and rescue helicopter

RH-3A Sea King
A mines countermeasures research helicopter

SH-3A Sea King
The initial version for the US and Japanese navies

CH-124A Sea King
The Canadian-built version

CH-3B Sea King
The export version known as the S-61A

CH-3C Pelican
A special enlarged version

Seen launching from the Italian carrier, Garibaldi, *this is the Agusta-built ASH-3D version of the S-61 Sea King series* (M. Gething).

SH-3D Sea King

Engines 2 × General Electric T58-GE-10 1,400 shp (max cont power 1,250 shp); **Crew** 2 pilots, 2 sonics operators; **Passengers** 12; **Max take-off weight** 9,300 kg (20,500 lb); **Payload** 3,918 kg (8,635 lb); **Empty weight** 5,382 kg (11,865 lb); **External load** 3,630 kg (8,000 lb); **Length** 16.69 m (54.75 ft); **Width** 4.98 m (16.33 ft); **Rotor diameter** 18.9 m (62 ft); **Height** 4.72 m (15.5 ft); **Max speed** 144 kt (267 km/h); **Max cruise speed** 118 kt (219 km/h); **Service ceiling** 4,480 m (14,700 ft); **Rate of climb** 11.2 m/sec (2,200 ft/min); **HIGE** 3,200 m (10,500 ft); **HOGE** 2,500 m (8,200 ft); **Range** 542 nm (1,005 km); **Weapons** (anti-submarine) 4 × Mk44/46 lightweight torpedoes, mines or depth bombs

VH-3D Sea King
The VIP transport

CH-3E Pelican
An SAR helicopter

HH-3E Jolly Green Giant

Engines 2 × General Electric T58-GE-5 1,500 shp (max cont power 1,250 shp); **Crew** 2 pilots, 1 flight engineer, 2 crewmen; **Passengers** 15-20; **Max take-off weight** 10,000 kg (22,050 lb); **Payload** 3,990 kg (8,795 lb); **Empty weight** 6,010 kg (13,255 lb); **Length** 17.45 m (57.25 ft); **Width** 4.82 m (15.81 ft); **Rotor diameter** as SH-3D; **Height** 4.9 m (16.07 ft); **Max speed** 141 kt (261 km/h); **Max cruise speed** 125 kt (232 km/h); **Service ceiling** 3,385 m (11,100 ft); **Rate of climb** 6.7 m/sec (1,310 ft/min); **HIGE** 1,250 m (4,100 ft); **HOGE** N A; **Range** 404 nm (748 km); **Weapons** (combat rescue) 2 × 7.62 mm mini-guns, grenade and smoke launchers

HH-3F Pelican

The long-range US Coast Guard helicopter

SH-3G Sea King

The updated ASW helicopter

SH-3H Sea King

The latest update

Agusta ASH-3 Sea King

The Italian-built series

Agusta S-61R

The last production variant of the Pelican

The Sea King has proved to be a most versatile and effective helicopter, built under licence by Agusta (still in production in the

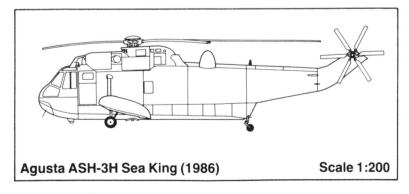

Agusta ASH-3H Sea King (1986)   **Scale 1:200**

ASH-3H and S-61R forms), by Mitsubishi (HSS-2 variant, still in production) and Westland (see separate entry). Although several nations are now looking for a Sea King replacement, recent deliveries of new airframes to Brazil and Venezuela prove there is still life in the helicopter yet.

The main US Naval role is the anti-submarine protection and rescue duties associated with an aircraft carrier task force, but the helicopter can be used for vertrep (re-supply) and even to carry troops as with the Argentine SH-3A Sea Kings during the Falklands crisis. The US Navy will replace its SH-3G/H models with the SH-60F Seahawk (see separate entry) in the late 1990s.

An enlarged and modified version, the HH-3 was designed for combat rescue duties in Vietnam and helicopters of this type now serve with USAF special operations units around the world, including Europe.

SIKORSKY S-62 SERIES

First flight 14 May 1958; **Operational** January 1963

S-62A Sea Guard
The export version

HH-52A Sea Guard

Engine 1 × General Electric T53-GE-8B 1,250 shp (max cont power 730 shp); **Crew** 2 pilots, 1 crewman; **Passengers** 11-12; **Max take-off weight** 3,764 kg (8,300 lb); **Payload** 1,459 kg (3,217 lb); **Empty weight** 2,305 kg (5,083 lb); **External load** 907 kg (2,000 lb); **Length** 13.58 m (44.55 ft); **Width** 3.7 m (12.1 ft); **Rotor diameter** 16.16 m (53 ft); **Height** 4.3 m (14.1 ft); **Max speed** 95 kt (175 km/h); **Max cruise speed** 85 kt (158 km/h); **Service ceiling** 3,414 m (11,200 ft); **Rate of climb** 5.5 m/sec (1,080 ft/min); **HIGE** 3,718 m (12,200 ft); **HOGE** 518 m (1,700 ft); **Range** 412 nm (764 km); **Weapons** unarmed

Designed to make use of the rotor dynamic components of the S-55 helicopter, the S-62 started life as a commercial development with a single turboshaft engine. It was quickly adopted by the US Coast Guard for short range recovery operations and eventually to operate at sea from Coast Guard cutters for ice patrol, rescue and the law enforcement role.

Operating with a Northrop FLIR system under test, this is a Los Angeles-based Sikorsky HH-52A Sea Guard helicopter of the USCG.

The US Coast Guard purchased 99 of the HH-52A Sea Guard model as a replacement for the H-34 (see separate entry) and based them around the Continental US (including Alaska), as well as on Puerto Rico and Hawaii. Since the late 1970s, these helicopters have proved to be exceptionally good at the role and have only started to be replaced by the HH-65A Dolphin (see separate entry for SA 365 series) since 1985. Even so, the airframes replaced have been drafted north to Alaska and the Great Lakes, as well as for embarked operations which will remain outside the scope of the Dolphin until a modification is completed in 1990.

Often called the single-engined Sea King, the Sea Guard was exported to India (none remain in service), Japan (where it continues a role with the Maritime Safety Agency) and Thailand (where it is reported to have been phased out of service).

The Sea Guard has a boat hull, with a large cabin capable of taking about ten or twelve survivors, often hoisted aboard by the nets and cradles carried by the helicopter. The two pilots fly the helicopter for the rescue operation, with the co-pilot acting as winch operator if the aircrewman is called upon to enter the water

Sikorsky HH-52A Sea Guard (1985) **Scale 1:125**

and assist survivors. Trials were carried out in 1983-85 with the Northrop forward looking infra-red system to assist in night time search operations where the person's heat would make his/her image stand out from the surrounding sea water or land. The trials proved the concept but the HH-52A will not be fitted with the system, its funding being reserved for the HH-65A in due course.

SIKORSKY S-65/S-80 SERIES

First flight 14 October 1964 (CH-53A), 13 December 1980 (CH-53E); **Operational** 1966 (CH-53A), 1983 (CH-53E)

Made under licence in Federal Germany, the CH-53G Stallion will remain in service with the Heeresflieger until the next century.

CH-53A Sea Stallion
The original version for the US Marine Corps

CH-53B Sea Stallion
A combat rescue helicopter

HH-53B Super Jolly
A USAF combat rescue version

CH-53D Sea Stallion
Engines 2 × General Electric T64-GE-413 3,925 shp; **Crew** 2 pilots, 1 flight engineer; **Passengers** 37 troops; **Max take-off weight** 19,068 kg (42,000 lb); **Payload** N A; **Empty weight** 10,662 kg (23,485 lb); **External load** N A; **Length** 20.47 m (67.17 ft); **Width** 4.72 m (15.5 ft); **Rotor diameter** 22.02 m (72.25 ft); **Height** 5.22 m (17.13 ft); **Max speed** 170 kt (315 km/h); **Max cruise speed** 150 kt (278 km/h); **Service ceiling** 6,401 m (21,000 ft); **Rate of climb** N A; **HIGE** 4,084 m (13,400 ft); **HOGE** 1,981 m (6,500 ft); **Range** 223 nm (413 km); **Weapons** unarmed

RH-53D Sea Stallion
The mines countermeasures version

CH-53E Super Stallion
Engines 3 × General Electric T64-GE-416 4,380 shp (max cont power 3,696 shp); **Crew** as CH-53D; **Passengers** 55; **Max take-off weight** 33,339 kg (73,500 lb); **Payload** 18,268 kg (40,274 lb); **Empty weight** 15,071 kg (33,226 lb); **External load** 14,619 kg (32,220 lb); **Length** 22.35 m (73.32 ft); **Width** 5.67 m (18.5 ft); **Rotor diameter** 24.08 m (79

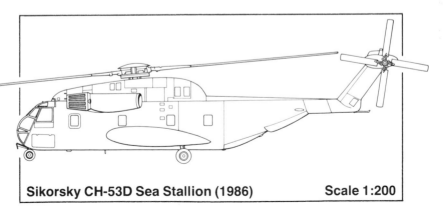

Sikorsky CH-53D Sea Stallion (1986)   **Scale 1:200**

Designed for aerial mines counter-measures work, this is the pre-production prototype of the huge Sikorsky MH-53E Sea Dragon.

ft); **Height** 5.66 m (18.56 ft); **Max speed and Max cruise speed** as CH-53D; **Service ceiling** 5,640 m (18,500 ft); **Rate of climb** 14 m/sec (2,750 ft/min); **HIGE** 3,520 m (11,550 ft); **HOGE** 2,895 m (9,500 ft); **Range** 1,120 nm (2,075 km); **Weapons** provision for 7.62 mm machine guns

MH-53E Sea Dragon
The new mines countermeasures version

VH-53F Sea Stallion
Cancelled

CH-53G Stallion
The German-built version

HH-53H Super Jolly
An enhanced special operations version

S-65C/O Stallion
An export version for Israel

S-80E Super Stallion
The export version of the CH-53E

The successful heavyweight from Sikorsky is the largest helicopter manufactured in the western world and has seen service in Vietnam, Grenada, Lebanon, Central America and with the Israeli defence forces during the various Arab-Israeli wars (including the famous 'liberation' of an Egyptian radar station). The helicopter has also been made under licence by Dornier-VFW-Fokker as the CH-53G for the Heeresflieger and it will remain in service until 2000 at least as the Bundeswehr's medium transport and night assault helicopter.

Sikorsky has designed, built and tested the three-engined Super Stallion which has now entered USMC and USN service ashore supporting the naval forces, including operations off Lebanon. Amongst the more impressive loads possible with this helicopter are 16 ton tracked combat vehicles and bulldozers.

The first production MH-53E Sea Dragon made its maiden flight in July 1986 and it will enter service in 1987-88 to replace the RH-53D fleet whose numbers were diminished by the abortive Teheran raid; ironically the Iranians operate a number of RH-53D supplied to the late Shah.

Production of the CH-53E and MH-53E will continue until about 1990 as the older variants are replaced in service.

SIKORSKY S-70A SERIES

First flight 17 October 1974 (YUH-60), 17 October 1978 (UH-60A); **Operational** June 1979 (UH-60A)

YUH-60
The prototype for the US Army competition

UH-60A Black Hawk
Engines 2 × General Electric T700-GE-700 1,560 shp; **Crew** 2 pilots, 1 aircrewman; **Passengers** 11-12; **Max take-off weight** 9,185 kg (20,250

Operated by the US Air Force to train pilots for more advanced versions, this UH-60A Black Hawk is identical to the US Army version.

lb); **Payload** 4,366 kg (9,626 lb); **Empty weight** 4,819 kg (10,624 lb); **External load** 3,629 kg (8,000 lb); **Length** 15.26 m (50.06 ft); **Width** 4.38 m (14.37 ft); **Rotor diameter** 16.36 m (53.67 ft); **Height** 3.76 m (11.33 ft); **Max speed** 195 kt (361 km/h); **Max cruise speed** 145 kt (269 km/h); **Service ceiling** 5,790 m (19,000 ft); **Rate of climb** 12.4 m/sec (2,450 ft/min); **HIGE** 2,896 m (9,500 ft); **HOGE** 3,170 m (10,400 ft); **Range** 324 nm (600 km); **Weapons** (trooping) 2 × 7.62 mm machine gun; (supplementary anti-tank) 16 × Hellfire laser-guided missiles

HH-60A Night Hawk
The USAF combat rescue helicopter programme

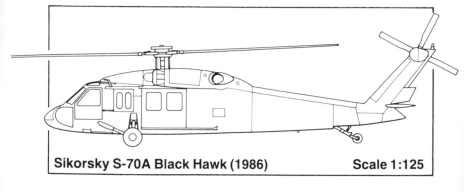

Sikorsky S-70A Black Hawk (1986)   **Scale 1:125**

For future combat rescue tasks, the Sikorsky HH-60A Night Hawk would seem to be the ideal helicopter; note the long-range tanks (Sikorsky).

EH-60A Quick Hawk
The Quick Fix II air vehicle

HH-60D Night Hawk
The all-weather combat rescue helicopter

HH-60E Night Hawk
An SAR helicopter project

S-70A Black Hawk
The export version for Australia and the Philippines

UH-60B Black Hawk
The updated utility version for the US Army

UH-60C Black Hawk
The projected growth version with new engines

Westland WS-70A
The proposed UK-built version for the RAF-British Army

A remarkable helicopter, the Black Hawk is now replacing the Bell UH-1 Huey (see separate entry) and has already been tested in action during Operation Fury (Grenada) in October 1983. The Black Hawk's pedigree goes back to the post-Vietnam competition to find a squad-carrier capable of surviving in 'hot' landing zones and being capable of transportation in USAF fixed-wing aircraft, such as the C-141.

By mid-1986 about 700 of the UH-60A series had been delivered to the US Army, with others in the USAF inventory with development versions planned to include the HH-60A Night Hawk programme for a combat rescue helicopter and the EH-60A special electronic missions aircraft, part of the Quick Fix programme. In US Army service a development programme has been carried out to prove the carrying of sixteen Hellfire missiles, but an outside laser designation source is required. The UH-60B version could be developed to provide 4,082 kg (9,000 lb) external load lifting for the new US Army Light Divisions with self-defence, chemical warfare and satellite navigation upgrades. The last UH-60A (number 1,108) is scheduled for mid-1990.

For the export market, the S-70A version has been ordered by the Philippines and Australia; it was selected by Spain and Switzerland but politically rejected. A Westland-built version has been offered to the RAF and could be powered by the RTM 322 engine, a flight test programme in a S-70C commercial variant was undertaken in 1986-87. Although there is the potential for some 300 Black Hawks in Europe, political considerations may make the Super Puma NH-90 (see separate entry) more likely. Nevertheless, the US Army has great faith in the helicopter which has been deployed to Korea, Panama, Honduras and Europe. In addition, it has taken place in various rapid deployment exercises.

SIKORSKY S-70B SERIES

First flight 12 December 1979; **Operational** 1984

SH-60B Seahawk

Engines 2 × General Electric T700-GE-401 1,713 shp; **Crew** 2 pilots, 2 sonics operators; **Passengers** 2; **Max take-off weight** 9,843 kg (21,700

Using the RAST haul-down system during trials, this is a fully equipped Sikorsky SH-60B Seahawk LAMPS-III air vehicle (Sikorsky).

lb); **Payload** 2,924 kg (6,446 lb); **Empty weight** 6,191 kg (13,648 lb); **External load** 2,268 kg (5,000 lb); **Length** 15.26 m (50.06 ft); **Width** 3.26 m (10.7 ft); **Rotor diameter** 16.36 m (53.67 ft); **Height** 3.79 m (12.45 ft); **Max speed** 145 kt (269 km/h); **Max cruise speed** 135 kt (249 km/h); **Service ceiling** 3,048 m (10,000 ft); **Rate of climb** 6.1 m/sec (1,192 ft/min); **HIGE and HOGE** N A; **Range** N A; **Weapons** (anti-submarine) 2 × Mk 46 lightweight torpedo, 1 × fuel tank; (surface search) 2 × Mk 46 torpedoes, 1 × Penguin anti-ship missile; (alternative) depth charges, mines

SH-60F Oceanhawk
The planned USN SH-3 replacement

S-70B Seahawk
The export version for Australia and Spain

S-70F Seahawk
The export version of an SH-3 replacement

Sikorsky S-70B-2 Seahawk (1987)   **Scale 1:200**

S-70J Seahawk
The Japanese version

Anti-submarine warfare in the US Navy has LAMPS (Light Airborne Multi-Purpose System) as an integral part of a task group's anti-submarine protection and anti-ship surveillance and targeting (soon to include the Kongsberg Penguin missile). The LAMPS-III air vehicle is the SH-60B Seahawk which has been designed for low operating costs and simple maintenance. The helicopter is not able to undertake independent action but can be used for SAR, medevac and vertrep operations. The USN requirement is in excess of 200 helicopters.

The Royal Australian Navy has acquired the S-70B-2 model, powered by the same T700 engines but with the MEL Super Searcher radar, to operate from its FFG-7 frigates for anti-submarine warfare. In addition, the Spanish Armada has ordered the helicopter for frigate operations and will use the same systems as the LAMPS-III model; as part of the acquisition arrangement, CASA of Madrid will be undertaking production of Seahawk components.

In Japan, the Seahawk has been selected for the HSS-X programme to find a new shipborne anti-submarine helicopter and part of the arrangement includes co-production. This model has been designated S-70J by Sikorsky.

To fulfil a need for the SH-3 Sea King replacement, Sikorsky has been contracted to develop a dipping sonar, 'inner zone' carrier-based version of the S-70, known as the SH-60F CV-HELO for service with the USN and (unarmed) with the US Coast Guard. This version could also be made available for export as a Sea King replacement and is a candidate for the Rolls-Royce/Turbomeca RTM 322-01 engine. Nations showing interest include the Netherlands, Brazil and Argentina.

The LAMPS-III air vehicle, operating from CCG-7 and other USN frigates, uses the Indal Technologies RAST haul-down system to ensure continued operations in bad weather conditions. The helicopter is attached to the ship's flight deck and at the right moment a ship-side operator reels in the landing helicopter; the system holds the helicopter on deck and permits movement to the hangar without crewmen on deck.

SIKORSKY S-76 SERIES

First flight 13 March 1977 (S-76A), April 1982 (AUH-76); **Operational** 1982

AUH-76
The military version of the S-76A civil helicopter

S-76A
The civil version used for military SAR and other duties

H-76B Eagle
Engines 2 × Pratt & Whitney PT6B-36 960 shp (max cont power 870 shp); **Crew** 2 pilots; **Passengers** 12; **Max take-off weight** 4,990 kg (11,000 lb); **Payload** 2,220 kg (4,850 lb); **Empty weight** 2,769 kg (6,150 lb); **External load** 1,500 kg (3,300 lb); **Length** 13.44 m (44 ft); **Width** 2.13 m (7 ft); **Rotor diameter** 13.41 m (44 ft); **Height** 4.42 m (14.5 ft); **Max speed** 155 kt (287 km/h); **Cruise speed** 145 kt (269 km/h); **Service ceiling** 4,828 m (16,000 ft); **Rate of climb** N A; **HIGE** 2,865 m (9,400 ft);

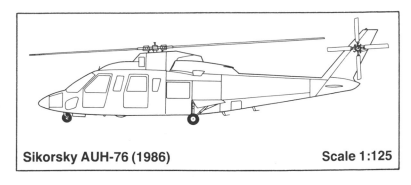

Sikorsky AUH-76 (1986)   **Scale 1:125**

Shown carrying an army jeep, the Sikorsky H-76 Eagle is a combat support helicopter which can be quick-changed into an attack helicopter (Sikorsky).

HOGE 1,768 m (5,800 ft); **Range** 353 nm (654 km); **Weapons** (anti-tank) 16 × TOW missiles (with mast-mounted sight); (armed reconnaissance) 2 × 4 TOW, 2 × 7.62 mm machine gun pods; (scout) 7.62 mm or 12.7 mm gun pods; (close support) 70 mm rocket pods

H-76N
The proposed naval version of the H-76A

Unique to the Sikorsky stable, the H-76/S-76 series was originally designed for the civil market in general and offshore transportation in particular. Initially Sikorsky tried to paint the helicopter olive drab and call it military but in 1985 it revealed the re-engined H-76 Eagle as an almost new, multi-mission helicopter.

The AUH-76 is also unique because in 1986 a flight of these helicopters from the Philippines Air Force was successful in providing cover for the new government of Mrs Aquino at a time when the coup seemed destined to fail. The Philippines had received a number of S-76s in the early 1980s. Other export users include Bahrain, Jordan and Brunei. Sikorsky tried to interest Belgium in the helicopter with a co-production agreement in 1985 but seemingly without success so far.

With 46 per cent more power, the H-76B Eagle seems certain to capture part of the growing multi-role helicopter market which fulfils the requirements of smaller nations who need an anti-tank, armed reconnaissance, scout and close support helicopter all in one. In addition the Eagle will undertake limited load lifting, casualty evacuation, combat re-supply, escort and infantry assault. Role change takes a matter of minutes according to the manufacturer. A stronger airframe, improved main and tail rotor transmission systems all give improved hot and high altitude performance which should make the helicopter attractive to Middle and Far Eastern nations. For trooping, the rear cabin can seat ten troops or carry twelve without seats but fully equipped; the cubic space is 5.8 cu m (204 cu ft) and underfuselage hook can cope with a light wheeled reconnaissance vehicle.

For the light shipborne role, Sikorsky has been offering the H-76N, equipped with Ferranti Sea Spray Mk III or MEL Super Searcher radar as a rival to the Westland Lynx (see separate entry). This version of the S-76 would carry anti-shipping missiles and lightweight torpedoes but lacking a processor system onboard is only a weapons carrier.

WESTLAND HELICOPTERS

WESSEX SERIES

First flight 17 May 1957 (Wessex 1), 31 May 1963 (Wessex 5);
Operational June 1960 (Mk 1), December 1963 (Mk 5)

Wessex HAS 1
The first variant

Wessex HC 2
Still operational with the Royal Air Force

Wessex HAS 3
The second ASW variant, retired 1984

Wessex HCC 4
The VIP transport for the Queen's Flight

Wessex HU 5

Engines 2 × Rolls-Royce Gnome 110 1,350 shp (max cont power 900 shp); **Crew** 1-2 pilots, 1 aircrewman; **Passengers** 12-13; **Max take-off weight** 6,124 kg (13,500 lb); **Payload** 2,197 kg (4,843 lb); **Empty weight** 3,927 kg (8,657 lb); **External load** 1,360 kg (3,000 lb); **Length** 14.7 m (48.4 ft); **Width** 3.7 m (12 ft); **Rotor diameter** 17.1 m (56 ft); **Height** 4.4 m (14.4 ft); **Max speed** 116 kt (214 km/h); **Max cruise speed** 105 kt (195 km/sec); **Service ceiling** 3,050 m (10,000 ft); **Rate of climb** 8.4 m/sec (1,650 ft/min); **HIGE** N A; **HOGE** 1,220 m (4,000 ft); **Range** 290 nm (538 km); **Weapons** generally unarmed but can mount 7.62 mm gun pod or 70 mm rocket pods; trials carried out with 4 × AS 11 wire-guided missiles

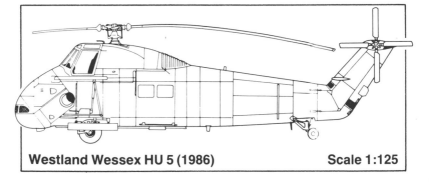

Westland Wessex HU 5 (1986)   **Scale 1:125**

Operated for SAR and Flag Officer duties only, the Westland Wessex HU 5 has served the Royal Navy well for over 25 years (RN/Culdrose).

Developed as a turbine-powered version of the Sikorsky S-58/H-34 series (see separate entry), the Westland Wessex series has faithfully served the Royal Navy and Royal Air Force for nearly three decades. Today, the helicopter has left front-line commando logical support service with the Fleet Air Arm and even in the SAR and Flag Officer support role, the helicopter will be phased out of service by 1990. The last front line unit was 845 Squadron at RNAS Yeovilton, Somerset, which unit played a significant part in the liberation of the Falkland Islands in 1982, including the vertical stores work at Ascension Island during the so-called roulement operation prior to the opening of Mount Pleasant airfield.

In the early 1980s, the Wessex HC 2 was redeployed from RAF Germany to support tasks in the United Kingdom and the helicopters are still operational in support of the British Army and Royal Ulster Constabulary in Northern Ireland where they continue to make a major contribution to the anti-terrorist war. A cost-effective and politically acceptable replacement seems doubtful in the short term. As part of a programme to equip several units for the Royal Auxiliary Air Force, some HU 5 versions were converted for air force service but these appear to have been moved into store.

Around the United Kingdom and in Cyprus, the Wessex SAR versions undertake sterling service primarily to rescue downed aircrew but also for all manner of humanitarian work, particularly rescue at sea and in co-ordination with the UK's Royal National Lifeboat Institution.

Overseas the terms of the licence agreement from Sikorsky rather limited export potential, but some helicopters were temporarily transferred to Bangladesh and Oman, others were delivered to Ghana. None of these appears to continue in operation.

WESTLAND SCOUT/WASP SERIES

First flight 1961 (Scout), 28 October 1962 (Wasp); **Operational** 1963 (Scout), 1964 (Wasp)

P 531
The prototype variant

Scout AH 1
The battlefield version

Wasp HAS 1

Engine 1 × Rolls-Royce Nimbus 710 shp; **Crew** 1 pilot, 1 aircrewman; **Passengers** 3; **Max take-off weight** 2,495 kg (5,500 lb); **Payload** 929 kg (2,048 lb); **Empty weight** 1,566 kg (3,452 lb); **External load** 680 kg (1,500 lb); **Length** 9.24 m (30.3 ft); **Width** 2.64 m (8.67 ft); **Rotor diameter** 9.83 m (32.25 ft); **Height** 2.72 m (8.92 ft); **Max speed** 104 kt (194 km/h); **Max cruise speed** 96 kt (177 km/h); **Service ceiling** 3,720 m (12,500 ft); **Rate of climb** 7.2 m/sec (1,440 ft/min); **HIGE** 3,720 m (12,500 ft); **HOGE** 2,682 m (8,800 ft); **Range** 263 nm (488 km); **Weapons** (anti-submarine) 2 × Mk 44 lightweight torpedoes, 2 × Mk 11 depth charges or 2 × mines; (anti-ship) 2 × AS 12 wire-guided missiles

The Scout/Wasp series was the first wholly British-designed light helicopter programme, originally conceived by Saunders-Roe, later part of the Westland Group. The Scout was originally designed as light observation and scout helicopter to supplement the ground reconnaissance forces for the British Army and as such it saw service in a number of theatres including Aden and Borneo. Later the Scout was used in the Falklands conflict for a range of tasks including casualty evacuation, reconnaissance, forward area re-supply, command and control and special forces insertion.

By the mid-1970s, it was obvious that armed helicopters were necessary to reduce the imbalance of Warsaw Pact to NATO main

An unusual shot of a Westland Wasp HAS 1 firing an AS 12 missile during a practice shoot; note the twin wire system (RN/Osprey).

battle tanks in the central region of Europe. The Scout was armed with the Nord AS/SS 11 wire-guided missile which uses a Ferranti direct view optical sight for aiming and tracking the missile. The Scout is no longer part of the British Army of the Rhine and has been withdrawn from service in Northern Ireland, but it is used by United Kingdom Land Forces aviation units and supports such groups as the garrisons in Hong Kong and the Falkland Islands, as well as the Territorial Army and the Special Air Service Regiment.

The world's first successful and operational small ship's helicopter was the Wasp which today remains in service with a limited number of older frigates and some survey ships of the Royal Navy. In the anti-submarine role, the Wasp carries various stores including two Mk 44 torpedoes which it drops as directed by the mother ship or controlling Sea King helicopter. During the liberation of South Georgia, Wasps from the frigate *Plymouth* and the Ice Patrol Ship *Endurance*, together with other helicopters, crippled the Argentine submarine *Santa Fe* with AS 12 missiles.

It is planned to phase out the Wasps from British service in 1988 and by 1987 the last remaining front-line Wasp unit, 829 Squadron will have been re-equipped with the Westland Lynx HAS 2/3 (see

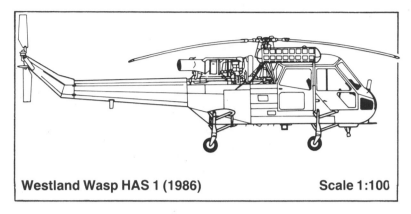

Westland Wasp HAS 1 (1986)   **Scale 1:100**

separate entry). Overseas the Wasp remains in service with the navies of Indonesia and Brazil, and with the South Africa Air Force Southern Air Command in Cape Town.

ARMY LYNX SERIES

First flight 21 March 1971 (Lynx Utility), 14 June 1984 (Lynx-3);
Operational December 1977 (Army Lynx)

A utility version of the Westland Lynx AH 1 collects a Milan anti-tank missile team from the battlefield during trials in the UK.

Yet to find a customer, the Westland Lynx-3 is nevertheless an impressive multi-role combat support helicopter; note Hellfire missiles.

Lynx AH 1

Engines 2 × Rolls-Royce Gem 41/43 1,000 shp (max cont power 890 shp); **Crew** 2 pilots; **Passengers** 10; **Max take-off weight** 4,535 kg (10,000 lb); **Payload** 1,565 kg (3,452 lb); **Empty weight** 2,970 kg (6,548 lb); **External load** 1,360 kg (3,000 lb); **Length** 13.3 m (43.63 ft); **Width** 3 m (9.84 ft); **Rotor diameter** 12.8 m (42 ft); **Height** 3.5 m (11.5 ft); **Max speed** 160 kt (296 km/h); **Max cruise speed** 140 kt (259 km/h); **Service ceiling** 3,658 m (12,000 ft); **Rate of climb** 12.3 m/sec (2,420 ft/min); **HIGE** N A; **HOGE** 3,230 m (10,600 ft); **Range** 340 nm (630 km); **Weapons** (anti-tank) 8 × TOW missiles or 8 × Hellfire; (close-support) SNEB or SURA rockets, 7.62 mm machine guns or 20 mm cannon; (self-defence) air-to-air missiles

Lynx AH 5
Development variant

Lynx AH 7
Announced in June 1985 as improved version

Lynx AH 28
The Qatar armed forces version

Lynx-2
The export version of the AH 7 (improved engines)

149

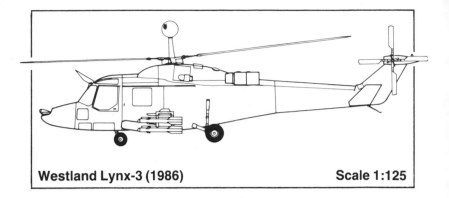

Westland Lynx-3 (1986)   **Scale 1:125**

Lynx-3

Engines 2 × Rolls-Royce Gem 60-3/2 1,180 shp (max cont power 1,150 shp); **Crew** 2 pilots; **Passengers** 9; **Max take-off weight** 5,897 kg (13,000 lb); **Payload** 2,494 kg (5,500 lb); **Empty weight** 3,379 kg (7,450 lb); **External load** 1,814 kg (4,000 lb); **Length** 15.24 m (50 ft); **Width** N A; **Rotor diameter** 12.8 m (42 ft); **Height** 3.3 m (10.83 ft); **Max speed** 161 kt (298 km/h); **Max cruise speed** 150 kt (278 km/h); **Service ceiling** 3,657 m (12,000 ft); **Rate of climb** 11.7 m/sec (2,300 ft/min); **HIGE** 1,463 m (4,800 ft); **HOGE** 914 m (3,000 ft); **Range** 373 nm (691 km); **Weapons** (anti-tank) 8 × Hellfire, HOT-2 or TOW-2; (close support) 2 × 20 mm Oerlikon guns or 2/4 × 70 mm rocket pods; (self-defence) combination including 12.7 mm chin-mounted Lucas turret and/or 4 × Stinger air-to-air missiles

Designed to meet a British Army requirement for a battlefield utility helicopter capable of taking a section of men to the forward area, the Lynx has been developed to take the Hughes Aircraft TOW anti-tank missile system with the British Aerospace roof sight for anti-armour operations in what the UK Army Air Corps calls HELARM — massed attack by helicopters in defensive positions. In a secondary role, the Lynx (without missiles) can carry two air mobile Milan anti-tank missile teams to ambush positions and re-supply them. The Lynx AH 1 is also operated by the Royal Marines for tasks in Norway.

The AH 5 is a single development variant but the new AH 7 has improved performance given by the Westland 30 (see separate entry) tail rotor system, allowing a higher all-up weight for the helicopter in the battlefield environment. The helicopter will also have a full night/day TOW sight capability, provision for the eventual fitting of self-defence missiles and/or countermeasures, radar warning receivers and laser designation.

In 1982, Westland announced the Lynx-3 project which although it has not interested the British Army has been looked at with interest overseas; at the time of writing no orders have been taken. The advanced design and systems of the Lynx-3 include the provision for Hellfire laser-guided missiles, heavier close support armament options, the use of the Racal Avionics management system, RAMS, to reduce the pilots' workload in the battlefield and a wheeled undercarriage for ease of handling and better force landing performance. Lynx-3 is not rated as an attack helicopter but as a multi-role or combat support helicopter.

In August 1986, the company demonstrator, G-LYNX, achieved the absolute world speed record of 216 kt (400 km/h).

NAVY LYNX SERIES

First flight 25 May 1972; **Operational** 1976

Lynx HAS 2
The first RN shipborne version

Lynx HAS 3
Engines 2 × Rolls-Royce Gem 41/43 1,000 shp (max cont power 890 shp); **Crew** 1 pilot, 1 observer, 1 aircrewman (optional); **Passengers** 8-9; **Max take-off weight** 4,876 kg (10,750 lb); **Payload** 1,766 kg (3,894 lb); **Empty weight** 3,110 kg (6,856 lb); **External load** 272 kg (600 lb); **Length** 10.61 m (34.83 ft); **Width** 2.04 m (9.64 ft); **Rotor diameter** 12.8

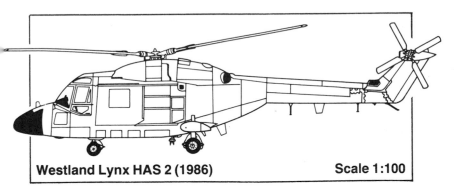

Westland Lynx HAS 2 (1986)   **Scale 1:100**

Called the Sea Lynx by the Federal German Navy, the Lynx Mk 88 has proved very successful in shipborne operations worldwide (Westland).

m (42 ft); **Height** 3.2 m (10.5 ft); **Max speed** 145 kt (269 km/h); **Max cruise speed** 125 kt (232 km/h); **Service ceiling** 3,658 m (12,000 ft); **Rate of climb** 11 m/sec (2,170 ft/min); **HIGE** N A; **HOGE** 2,556 m (7,400 ft); **Range** 320 nm (593 km); **Weapons** (anti-ship) 4 × Sea Skua missiles; (anti-submarine) 2 × Mk 44/Mk 46/Stingray lightweight torpedoes, or Mk 11 depth charges or mines

Lynx Mk 2

The French naval version with dipping sonar

Lynx Mk 4

The French-equipped version

Lynx HAS 8

The uprated version for the RN with 360° radar

Lynx Mk 21

The Brazilian version

Lynx Mk 23

The Argentine version

Lynx Mk 25

The Dutch SAR version (UH-14A)

Lynx Mk 27
The Dutch dipping sonar version (SH-14A)

Lynx Mk 80
The Danish naval version

Lynx Mk 81
The Dutch MAD-equipped version (SH-14B)

Lynx Mk 86
The Norwegian coastguard version

Lynx Mk 87
The export version not delivered

Lynx Mk 88
The German naval version

Lynx Mk 89
The Nigerian naval version

Super Lynx
The export version of the HAS 8

A replacement for the Wasp (see separate entry), the Lynx has proved to be an excellent naval helicopter with considerable export potential. Production is destined to continue until at least 1989 and so far some sixty helicopters are in service with the Royal Navy flying from frigates, destroyers and the Ice Patrol Ship; HRH Prince Andrew is a qualified Lynx helicopter weapons instructor.

Today the main Royal Navy role for the helicopter is anti-shipping using the Sea Skua missile which was first used operationally in the Falklands conflict. In some Type 22 frigate flights, two Lynx are carried to allow for sustained defence against enemy surface craft, but of course the helicopter is equally able to drop ASW weapons although in the Royal Navy it currently lacks a processor to deal with sonobuoy operations and needs outside guidance. In the surface search role, the Lynx HAS 2/3 is equipped with the Ferranti Sea Spray radar and Racal Orange Crop electronic surveillance measures; the Lynx HAS 8 will also have a new 360° radar and GEC Avionics Sea Owl passive identification system, both mounted on the nose. The German Navy is currently improving its fleet as well.

Export successes have included the Argentine Navy which used its Lynx to assault Port Stanley in 1982, leading to the cancellation of the Mk 87.

SEA KING SERIES

First flight 7 May 1969 (HAS 1); **Operational** February 1970

Sea King HAS 1
The first British version

Sea King HAS 2
The improved version, superceded by the HAS 5

Sea King AEW 2
The airborne early warning version

Operating afloat is rare these days for the Royal Australian Navy's Sea King Mk 50 force from 817 Squadron, as they have no carrier (PEB).

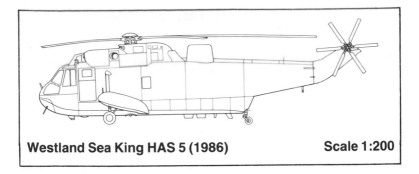

Westland Sea King HAS 5 (1986) Scale 1:200

Sea King HAR 3
The specialist RAF SAR version

Sea King HAS 5

Engines 2 × Rolls-Royce Gnome H1400-1 1,660 shp (max cont power 1,250 shp); **Crew** 2 pilots, 1 observer, 1 sonar operator/aircrewman; **Passengers** 12; **Max take-off weight** 9,526 kg (21,000 lb); **Payload** 3,629 kg (8,000 lb); **Empty weight** 5,896 kg (13,000 lb); **External load** 3,400 kg (7,500 lb); **Length** 17.01 m (55.8 ft); **Width** 4.98 m (16.33 ft); **Rotor diameter** 18.9 m (62 ft); **Height** 4.91 m (16.3 ft); **Max speed** 144 kt (267 km/h); **Max cruise speed** 112 kt (208 km/h); **Service ceiling** 3,200 m (10,500 ft); **Rate of climb** 10.3 m/sec (2,020 ft/min); **HIGE** 1,525 m (5,000 ft); **HOGE** 975 m (3,200 ft); **Range** 664 nm (1,230 km); **Weapons** (anti-submarine) 4 × Mk 46/Stingray lightweight torpedo, or 4 × Mk 11 depth charges; (anti-ship) 4 × Sea Skua (Federal German Navy) or 2 × Sea Eagle (Indian Navy)

Sea King HAS 6
The proposed advanced version for the RN

Sea King Mk 41
The German naval version

Sea King Mk 42 series
For the Indian Navy

Sea King Mk 43
The Norwegian SAR version

Sea King Mk 45
The Exocet-armed Pakistani version

Sea King Mk 47
The Egyptian version

Sea King Mk 48
The Belgian SAR/VIP version

Sea King Mk 50
The Australian version

Developed directly from the Sikorsky SH-3 Sea King (see separate entry), the British-built medium ASW helicopter has been developed to the HAS 5 stage which is now reckoned to be the best of its class in the world. Today, the Sea King HAS 5 operates from the 'Invincible' Class aircraft carriers and Royal Fleet Auxiliary ships of the Royal Navy, as well as supporting the Falkland Islands protection zone. It uses a Plessey dipping sonar and sonobuoys to detect submarines.

In 1982, following the loss of warships to sea-skimming missile attack in the South Atlantic, the British MoD and Westland with Thorn-EMI Electronics developed the AEW 2 version in a matter of weeks. This uses the HAS 2 airframe with the Searchwater radar radome attached to the starboard side of the helicopter. The radar system, with two observer/controllers is supported by the Racal Orange Crop and Cossor Jubilee Guardsman electronic warfare systems. One squadron is now in commission, but the Search-water has been sold to Spain and is being studied by India and Italy.

Export versions include the Sea King Mk 45 for Pakistan, armed with the French Exocet missile and the newer Mk 42B with the MEL Super Searcher radar and the provision of the Sea Eagle anti-shipping missile, making the helicopter into a mini-frigate. Federal Germany's Navy began trials with the British Aerospace Sea Skua missile system for the Sea King Mk 41 in 1986. Several users have ordered replacement uprated engined versions for fleet enhancement and to replace attrition losses. Westland hopes to continue with the Advanced Sea King (the export HAS 8) until the development of the EH 101 (see separate entry) in 1990.

COMMANDO SERIES

First flight 12 September 1973 (Commando Mk 1), September 1979 (Sea King HC 4); **Operational** 1975 (Commando Mk 1); November 1979 (Sea King HC 4)

Commando Mk 1
The transport version for Egypt

Commando Mk 2
The improved version for Egypt

Commando Mk 2A
The Qatari version

Commando Mk 2B
The VIP version for Egypt

Seen prior to delivery, a VIP configured Westland Commando Mk 2B of the Egyptian Air Force operated on behalf of the country's government.

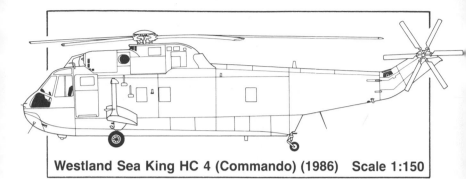

Westland Sea King HC 4 (Commando) (1986)   Scale 1:150

Commando Mk 2C
The VIP version for Qatar

Commando Mk 2E
The electronic warfare version for Egypt

Commando Mk 3
The armed version for Qatar

Sea King HC 4

Engines 2 × Rolls-Royce Gnome H 1400-1T 1,660 shp (max cont power 1,250 shp); **Crew** 1-2 pilots, 1 aircrewman; **Passengers** 21 (assault), 28 (short-range); **Max take-off weight** 9,525 kg (21,000 lb); **Payload** 3,825 kg (8,434 lb); **Empty weight** 5,700 kg (12,566 lb); **External load** 3,400 kg (7,500 lb); **Length** 17.02 m (55.83 ft); **Width** 3.96 m (13 ft); **Rotor diameter** 18.9 m (62 ft); **Height** 4.91 m (16.3 ft); **Max speed** 125 kt (232 km/h); **Max cruise speed** 112 kt (208 km/h); **Service ceiling** 1,525 m (5,000 ft); **Rate of climb** 10.3 m/sec (2,020 ft/sec); **HIGE** 1,525 m (5,000 ft); **HOGE** 975 m (3,200 ft); **Range** 240 nm (445 km); **Ferry range** 664 nm (1,230 km); **Weapons** 2 × 7.62 mm door-mounted machine guns; (Qatar) 2 × Exocet missiles; (Egypt) 4 × AS 12 missiles

Produced as a direct result of an Egyptian order for a support helicopter to supplement the Soviet-built Mil Mi-8 (see separate entry) transports which were being grounded through lack of spares immediately after the Russian withdrawal. The Commando Mk 1 was an interim design, joined a couple of years later by the Mk 2 with room for 28 troops, again using the same Sea King HAS 2 (see separate entry) fuselage without the ASW equipment and now continuing troop seating. The Mk 2E is equipped with

Italian-designed electronic countermeasures equipment and the four helicopters delivered are thought to be operational on the Egyptian border with Libya. The Mk 3 is equipped with the Aerospatiale Exocet missile.

In 1979, the Royal Navy ordered the helicopter to supplement and eventually replace the Wessex HU 5 (see separate entry) in support of the Royal Marines during amphibious operations and re-supply operations. During the Falklands conflict (1982), the helicopter was used for assault, transportation of freight and men, special operations and re-supply between ships. Many hundreds of thousands of pounds of *materiel* was moved in this way and the helicopter earned a fine reputation during the conflict. One of the more interesting facets was the arrival of a single Sea King HC 4 on Chilean soil and it is thought that the operation was either to land an SAS/SBS team for sabotage on the Argentine mainland or a specially-arranged spoof to draw attention away from the San Carlos landings. In 1984, the Sea King HC 4 was involved in the rescue of civilians from Beirut. The Sea King HC 4 replaced the Wessex HU 5 in 1986, is now operated by 845, 846 and 707 Squadrons based at RNAS Yeovilton, Somerset but also supporting the Royal Marines in Norway and elsewhere. Trials are also being carried out with night vision goggles and other equipment.

WESTLAND 30 SERIES

First flight 10 April 1979

W30-60
A commercial variant

W30-100-60
A commercial variant

W30-300
The General Electric powered version

TT30
Engines 2 × Rolls-Royce Gem 60-3/2 1,180 shp; **Crew** 1-2 pilots, 1 aircrewman; **Passengers** 14-16; **Max take-off weight** 5,806 kg (12,800

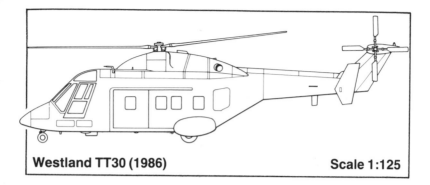

Westland TT30 (1986)　　　　　**Scale 1:125**

lb); **Payload** 2,501 kg (5,514 lb); **Empty weight** 3,305 kg (7,286 lb); **External load** 2,268 kg (5,000 lb); **Length** 14.7 m (46.7 ft); **Width** 3.1 m (10.2 ft); **Rotor diameter** 13.3 m (43.6 ft); **Height** 4.74 m (15.6 ft); **Max speed** 138 kt (256 km/h); **Max cruise speed** 125 kt (232 km/h); **Service ceiling** 3,048 m (10,000 ft); **Rate of climb** 11.9 m/sec (2,350 ft/min); **HIGE** 808 m (2,650 ft); **HOGE** 701 m (2,300 ft); **Range** 346 nm (641 km); **Weapons** 2 × 7.62 mm door-mounted machine guns

W30-404

The proposed version for RAF. **Max take-off weight** 8,165 kg (18,000 lb); **Payload** 2,650 kg (5,843 lb); **Cruise speed** 150 kt (278 km/h); **Range** 265 nm (490 km)

Although it has not been a success in the commercial helicopter market, except for the examples leased by Pan American and 21 sold to India, the W30 is still being developed for a possible military helicopter market. The helicopter was however said to have precipitated the 1985-86 Westland crisis which ironically led Westland into an agreement to develop the Sikorsky S-70A Black Hawk (see separate entry) which has been its rival for the RAF Puma/Wessex replacement requirement, known as AST 404. The W30-404 is the version optimized for this role with troop transportation, logistical re-supply and casualty evacuation as the primary roles, and SAR, communications, command and control and aerial mine laying as the second tasks.

The W30-404 has been designed to have a good pilot working environment with management avionics systems, good external visibility, night vision compatibility and an automatic flight control system. In the rear cabin, the design takes into consideration the

Approaching a tight field landing sight, the Westland 30 has still to attract any orders despite its obvious abilities (Westland).

need for troops to disembark rapidly and uses two large main doors with head room inside suitable for most fully-armed troops. The cabin seats fourteen fully-equipped infantrymen or takes over twenty troops without seats in battlefield conditions. For casualty evacuation, the helicopter can carry six stretchers, eight seated wounded and their attendants. For re-supply, the cargo hook can accommodate a light gun, ammunition and other freight. An electronic warfare and command post version could be developed because the spacious cabin can accommodate the necessary consoles, 'black boxes' and operators, with the fuel efficient RTM 322 or T700 engines giving over two hours endurance.

The TT30 has been marketed in Europe, Africa and the Far East but was not successful in Norway and Zimbabwe, however it is still reportedly in the running for a possible troop transport order from Sweden. The fact that Westland brought the W30 to the Farnborough Air Show in 1986, some several months after the Sikorsky rescue bid, emphasized the continued confidence in the helicopter.

THE MILITARY HELICOPTER'S FUTURE POTENTIAL

By the year 2010, the US Army intends to replace the existing 22 types of helicopter with just six types, including the two versions of the LHX (Light Helicopter Experiment) family, initially the LHX-SCAT (SCout ATtack) and the LHX-U (Utility) which should enter service in 1995 with a requirement for at least 5,000 machines. The LHX is the US Army's greatest peacetime programme and it again emphasizes the role of the helicopter on the modern battlefield. Supporting the LHX will be the CH-47D Chinook (to be replaced from 2000 by the ACH-XX design), the UH-60 Black Hawk (by then at B or C model), the AH-64 Apache (certainly to be updated to B or C standard) and the OH-58D Aeroscout; the last Cobra will have left service in 2005 and the last UH-1 Huey in 2007.

The US Army is banking heavily on the advanced technology of fly-by-light, composite construction, advanced controls and systems to give the LHX a single pilot capability thus allowing every crew seat to be filled at least by one pilot, preferably by a statistical 1.5 pilots to enable the demographic changes in American society and the 24-hour battle to be taken in account. The helicopter will fly at about 200 kt (370 km/h) which is the maximum speed thought possible with a conventional rotor system and the development costs of composite rotors, X-wing or tilt-rotor were thought too great for this programme.

The US Navy has however been a little more adventurous with the V-22 tilt-rotor design, known provisionally as JVX (Joint service air Vehicle Experiment), which has been described in the specifications section. Although Bell did propose the tilt-rotor for LHX, the design was not accepted by the (US) Department of the Army. At Sikorsky work is continuing with the X-wing project, sponsored by the US Army and NASA, and which first flew in early 1987 to prove the concept of vertical lift being provided by rotors which are stowed and become the airfoil lift bodies for a conventional aircraft, thus allowing greater forward speeds to be gained. This is obviously the way to the future for the military helicopter.

In Europe, the planned future developments are less spectacu-

Above *One of the possible configurations for the US Army's futuristic LHX programme comes from Boeing-Sikorsky's First Team and features a French-designed fenestron tail rotor system. The other contender is the Bell-McDonnell-Douglas SuperTeam. The helicopter should fly by 1990.*

Below *Really into the future, although the prototype has already flown, the Sikorsky/NASA X-Wing project shows the way in which rotorcraft may have to go as the limits of the conventional helicopter appear to have been reached already, especially in terms of speed (Sikorsky).*

lar but not lacking in technology. The realization that an individual company cannot spend the vast non-recurring sums required for research and development work has led to the Tonal project to develop a Light Attack Helicopter for Britain, Italy, the Netherlands and Spain as well as to the NH90 NATO-inspired idea to provide a medium helicopter for battlefield and naval roles by 2000 when many second generation helicopters will be phased out.

France and the Federal Republic of Germany had spent some time working on the Eurocopter PAH-2 project, the generic name for the third generation anti-tank helicopter for the Heeresflieger (PAH-2) and the ALAT (HAC-3G), with the addition of the close support and anti-helicopter helicopter (HAP) for France. The programme began running into difficulties in 1985 and was quietly re-defined in 1986, leaving the French and the Germans to develop a common airframe known as CATH.

In the Soviet Union, the third and possibly the fourth helicopter development phases are under way in what has been called the 'new defensive revolution' of that most air-minded government. Included in these designs have been the uprated Mi-24/25 assault helicopters, the Mi-17 re-engined from the Mi-8, the newly developed Mi-34 training/armed reconnaissance helicopter and

Part of a Franco-German design effort, the PAH-2 was another European joint venture to provide a future attack helicopter for the 1990s and beyond. The French version was called HAC and it has an anti-helicopter variant called HAP which should have been in service by 1990 (MBB).

An artist's impression of a future US Marine Corps assault using the V-22A Osprey, supported by the CH-53E Super Stallion and fixed-wing aircraft. Note the Osprey's tilt-rotor operation (Bell-Boeing).

the possibility of two tilt-rotor projects on paper — one for a twelve to fourteen seat Hind replacement and the other for a thirty to forty seat equivalent to the V-22 Osprey programme in the United States. It seems that the anti-helicopter role of the Mi-28 has been mirrored by the Ka-34 (Hokum) and one may be dropped before the end of the decade in order to fully develop the other for the battlefields of the next century when the Soviets believe that any future conflict will include large numbers of helicopters.

Elsewhere in the world there are a number of nations developing military helicopter manufacturing and development industries, including Australia, Belgium, Brazil, Canada, China (People's Republic), Egypt, India, Indonesia and Turkey. They have all borrowed from western technology, particularly from Bell, MBB and Sikorsky but with today's high costs of production, a licence for overseas work can ensure a production line for longer thus bringing down the product's unit cost to the home buyer. Sometimes the transfer of technology worries the NATO governments, especially when they see direct copies (with improvements) of western equipment such as the Mi-28/Apache and Mi-34/AS 350 Squirrel but overall the continued development of the worldwide helicopter industry has to be a welcome sign for the future of the military helicopter.